work
SMART

Your Formula
For UNPRECEDENTED
Professional Success

MARISA MURRAY

"Working harder isn't the answer; it's the problem." Forbes

Author: Marisa Murray
Editor: Daphne Parsekian
Cover design: Zeljka Kojic
Layout: Ida Fia Sveningsson

ISBN: 1978188684
ISBN-13: 978-1978188686

DEDICATION

This book is dedicated to all of the teachers in my life,
beginning with my parents (Norm and Rene), my sisters (Jacqui, Mimi,
Steph, and Chris), my husband (Paul), and my precious little gurus
(Toby and Theo).

TABLE OF CONTENTS

DOWNLOAD THE AUDIOBOOK FOR FREE!

READ THIS FIRST

Just to say thanks for buying my book,
I would like to give you the audiobook version

100% FREE!

Go to **www.leaderley.com/WorkSmartAudio**
to download.

FOREWORD

In today's workforce, most people feel obligated to work hard. Working hard is assumed to be correlated with delivering results, meeting deadlines, and overcoming obstacles. But is it really?

While working hard is seen by many as an obligation, working smarter (in a more effective and sustainable way) remains completely optional and up to you.   In fact, many people spend the better part of their careers working way too hard without any of their colleagues even noticing. I mean, when was the last time someone at your work sat you down to brainstorm making your job easier, more enjoyable or offered up ideas to help you work less?

But there is a proven formula for working smart that accelerates your success and creates much more ease and enjoyment in your work.

This book for ambitious professionals who want to learn to work smarter (not harder) to accelerate and progress in their careers. The book exposes common beliefs, habits, and behaviours that erode your performance, thus forcing you to work harder.

This WORK SMART formula covers the nine competency areas that you must master to excel and enjoy your professional life.

When properly implemented, the WORK SMART formula unleashes your ambition and motivation, taps into incremental determination and passion for your work — providing you with everything you need to take your performance to the next level but with much less effort.

I spent over 20 years in advancing leadership roles in corporate America working hard to get ahead. But my best years, were never my hardest.

Despite being exposed to the best professional development and coaching programs on the market, I noticed that I was often persuaded to apply an effort-based approach that included more hours, more stress and more fatigue. Some of these techniques temporarily enabled my ascension to leadership positions but it was not sustainable. Over time, my performance and satisfaction eroded when I relied on working way too hard.

What I discovered first hand, is that much of the advice I received was extremely ineffective at enabling my best work. And now as an executive coach for top leaders, I notice many of my clients repeating and propagating these exhausting practices. They are unconsciously modelling the misguided behavioural patterns embedded in too many of our corporate cultures. A pattern, that can stop with you.

By now thousands of corporate executives, professionals, and entrepreneurs have already benefited from adopting WORK SMART practices in their approach to their work.

Like Madhavi Mantha, a partner of Technology Strategy at Deloite Consulting who said: "The tools provided in this book are so practical, applicable, and relevant that I apply them every day."

This book contains the solutions and approaches you need to create meaningful and enjoyable work. I promise that if you apply these principles, you will achieve your goals and be flooded with new opportunities beyond your wildest dreams.

Now, I know you are busy, but don't miss out on the opportunity to significantly improve your experience at work. Investing in enjoying your work is the best gift you can give yourself. The impact of this framework is transformative—you will not regret it, and everyone will notice and want to know your secret.

The WORK SMART formula has proven to have positive, long-lasting results for my clients. All you have to do to tune your capabilities is to keep on reading. Each chapter will give you new insights as you master your new work habits.

Take action right now, and claim your next level of success! This book provides your roadmap to transform into the thriving leader you long to be, achieving unprecedented results and unlocking new opportunities for you and your organization.

INTRODUCTION

When I was pressed about why I was quitting this amazing job, I had no logical answer. I could only say, **"I'm unhappy. I've realized that my formula isn't working for me anymore, and I need to change it."**

On a date with my husband at a wonderful sushi restaurant on a Sunday evening in late May 2015, I looked up at him and smiled as my favourite champagne was being poured into my glass. We were celebrating my performance bonus, a fairly routine ritual as my career progression continued to surprise and delight us with prestige, perks, and cash.

As we clinked our glasses and sipped our bubbly, he said: "Hey, you seem a little sad."

I began by denying it, explaining that I was fine but just a little preoccupied with a number of derailing projects on my plate and eager for my transformation initiative to yield the benefits I knew it would.

He laughed and said, "Marisa, you always deliver. I know you—you will get the right team in place, inspire the heck out of them, and together you will transform the place."

I knew he was right. I thought, *In 12–18 months, I'm not going to recognize this division.* But what I said out loud shocked my husband. "Yeah, I guess I just wish I could fast forward and skip the next 18 months of my life. I don't feel like doing this anymore."

My husband's reaction surprised me. I didn't think I had said anything irrational; I was just being practical. But he put his glass down and said, **"You want to wish the next 18 months of our lives away?"**

I defended my position. "Well, not all of our lives...just the work part...you know, until I implement the changes I know they need."

"Do you really mean that?" he asked.
"Kind of," I answered sheepishly.

"If you want to wish away your life, my life, and the incredible and precious little time we have with our kids—then you should quit!"

When he said it, it felt like a lightbulb turned on in me. It had frankly never occurred to me to quit. I wasn't a quitter; I sought out new challenges and secured my next promotion. That always required delivering on my existing programs and never involved quitting on anyone.

But something just clicked in me. So I quit the very next day.

Humming Johnny Paycheck's famous line: "take this job and shove it, I ain't working here no more", I announced my departure to my boss. But I'll never forget what he said: "I'm sorry to hear that Marisa. I'm sure you've given this a lot of thought."

Then I burst into tears when I told my team. I felt awful for abandoning them, especially the new talent I had just brought into the organization. It was so difficult. I tried to reassure them about their futures, telling them I knew that they would make me proud, and I promised to somehow make them proud. Even though, I had no idea how or even where I would go next.

After a few more days, the confusion set-in. What did I just do? I threw away financial security for my family, a boatload of perks and a spotless career track record! What had happened to me? It was this last question that led me to the library. Sitting on the floor in the leadership development and career section, pulling out every book. Like a mad scientist, rummaging through data, trying to find a trend. Determined to figure out what I had missed.

In the months that followed, I was on a mission. I studied everything I could about human performance and leadership. I secretly enrolled in a number of executive coaching certification programs for the sole purpose of figuring myself out. Then one day, I realized that I had fallen in love (the coaching techniques, the neurosciences and the psychology of success). I could now see it, the many powerful concepts that I had overlooked.

I had worked with three executive coaches myself over the previous decade so I was stunned by the real potential in these teachings. Powerful concepts that I wasn't able to grasp during my programs but that now I understood, and knew could make a big difference to leaders. I set-out to serve real people, in the real world with their real-time challenges. In the trenches, working one-on-one and with their teams I began to catch glimpses of what worked and how I could make these abstract tools and concepts accessible, relevant and practical. I was now focused on one question: **What's the formula?**

Despite being educated at top schools, employed by top employers, and reaching leadership ranks (and the top 1% in record time) I had missed something. I was determined to find the real deal—the patterns, behaviours, and practices that *sustainably, predictably, and more easily* supported people in achieving the success and fulfillment, that ambitious-people-like-me desired. And once I did, I was going to share it with everyone I could.

The Formula Revealed...

What I came to discover is that many of the underlying beliefs, practices and even some of our basic understanding of business and career success need an upgrade—a more inspiring and complete one, that takes into account all of our human needs and taps into our greatest capabilities. This book provides that formula: The WORK SMART formula. The methods, tools and tricks that will spare you from a great deal of suffering. The formula contains 9 competencies and 50 skills that I wish I had better understood and applied more often. It is packed with practical examples that make the neuroscience and psychology of human performance understandable and highly relevant to you.

It is now my mission to help my clients avoid unnecessary or dramatic career changes by instead empowering them to proactively steer their professional endeavors towards the success and fulfilment they desire. My hope is that during this process you will shed your addiction to hard work and be open to new ways of thinking and acting that will create much more ease, unlocking your ability to achieve unimaginable success.

How to Dive In

Now I know you're busy, but every chapter is important; each one reveals an important aspect of the WORK SMART formula. All together they are transformative, but the order doesn't matter— feel free to dive in anywhere you want. If you want help deciding where to focus, you can go to **www.leaderley. com/WorkSmartAssessment** and take the skills assessment. Your personalized results can serve as your guide to the most relevant chapters for you.

Just keep reading, whether you are at the beginning of your career, or you are an experienced leader; whether you are an entrepreneur or individual contributor in an organization; this book has tools for you. Keep on reading, you won't regret it.

W WELL

O OPPORTUNITY-ORIENTED

R RELATIONSHIP-DRIVEN

K KIND

S SUCCESSFUL

M MANAGERIAL

A ACTION-ORIENTED

R RESILIENT

T TENACIOUS

WELL

Being Well - The Foundation

Are you well? Because you will do your best work when you are well. We are the best leaders, we are better colleagues, we are more focused, we are better at problem solving, and we are more creative when we are well.

The problem is that most of us are not very good at recognizing when we are not well.

It's funny because it is often obvious to everyone else.

I'll never forget being the only woman partner at our regional office on a panel during an all-employee town hall. The seven office partners were on stage taking questions from the audience. We received some great questions about the business and some challenging ones about the strategic direction of the firm, but overall, I left the stage feeling excited and proud of the talented people I worked with.

After the session, I caught up with my team to see if they had enjoyed the discussion as much as I had. To my surprise, they were not at all focused on the content of the discussion. They were distracted by how exhausted we all looked.

"You all look so overworked and tired...not a very inspiring sight" pretty much summarized the key take-away from the session.

Of course, it wasn't the kindest of comments, but I knew that it was also probably true. Apart from wishing I had worn more make-up; their input wasn't immediately actionable for me. I promised myself to wear mascara at the next event and I brushed it off.

What Well Looks Like

In retrospect, I cringe at some of the memories—the times when I barely had time to dry my hair, rushing my kids to daycare, lugging my fashionable but impractical overstuffed leather briefcase, and practically throwing out my back while balancing my cold coffee as I hustled in my high-heeled shoes to the client site.

I was a pretty unbalanced mess, but it all seemed normal at the time. I had the kind of health that was easy to take for granted. I was rarely sick, and when I was, it just meant I needed to have Advil Cold & Flu on hand—but I never let my body stop me from going to work.

People who struggle with their health are not so sloppy with themselves. Their body forces them to pay attention and slow down, but mine only gave me subtle clues.

The Symptoms

I was mostly grumpy with the people I loved. Tired and unable to function without coffee, I was extremely high strung with it. I couldn't relate to anyone who wasn't moving as fast as I was, and I was unbelievably impatient if anyone kept me waiting for anything.

But no one ever told me that being grumpy, impatient, and high strung meant that I was unwell. That's pretty much how everyone else around me behaved and looked.

II had to stop using my faulty gauge of how well I thought I felt and replace it instead with a more objective criteria. We all get used to chronic low-grade physical and emotional suffering, which makes us unreliable when it comes to determining if we are truly well.

What I will share with you in the first practice in the WORK SMART formula will not be new to you. Conceptually, I knew it too. Everyone knows that taking care of yourself is important, but we often neglect it because it is not urgent. I also neglected it for another reason. I neglected my wellness because it was in competition with the amount of time I could spend working. I could skip these rituals and work longer and harder, and I falsely believed that this would drive a good outcome.

The highest performing humans do not see their wellness rituals as being in competition with their work activities. They see them as critical to their success.

Once I realized the link between my wellness rituals and my success, everything changed for me, and it was upside from there.

So let's get specific: For human beings to be well enough to enjoy unprecedented success, there are five mandatory rituals. These rituals must be present in your life every single week (every day is best, but three to five times per week minimally).

Mandatory Wellness Rituals

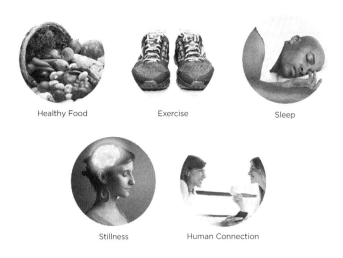

Healthy Food   Exercise   Sleep

Stillness   Human Connection

As we step through each of these areas one by one, I want you to objectively gauge your current baseline performance. You will be excited to hear that there is a significant upside to your career and life by tuning up these rituals.

Wellness Ritual #1: Healthy Food

Reflecting on our relationship with food can be a long and complicated exercise. We are often locked in some sort of twisted power struggle with our bodies. Alternating between overindulgence (leading to weight gain) and deprivation (to lose that weight) and intermixed with all the emotional eating to deal with our daily challenges or to celebrate our triumphs, our food choices are rarely solely about nutrition.

Most professionals' daily food habits include lots of coffee, breads, pastas, baked goods, sugars, candy, and alcohol. These foods provide us with comfort, and they fill us up while they distract our busy selves from eating sufficient amounts of high-nutrient foods.

Don't get me wrong—I'm sure you eat healthy-ish foods—I bet you order a pizza covered in vegetables instead of meat—but the reality of working hard is that you are often in a rush and reach for whatever is accessible. Unfortunately, these most convenient food items are often far too high in refined carbohydrates and deficient in many vital nutrients.

Research published in the American Journal of Clinical Nutrition confirmed a significant increase in our consumption of high glycemic-index foods when studying the daily food intake of nearly 350,000 people over a period of 23 years.[1] This increase correlated with many negative health outcomes including yo-yo effects in our blood sugar, producing inflammation and damaging our body's insulin sensitivities. As if this isn't bad enough, these eating habits also hurt our brains. Specifically, the Harvard Mahoney Neuroscience Institute found that excess glucose also causes memory loss and cognitive deficiencies. [2]

This begs the question: "If we're not eating to provide our bodies with the nutrients it needs, what are we eating for?"

I would love to say pleasure and taste, which usually played a part in the moment of choice, but the truth is that most of the time I was eating so fast that the food was completely unpalatable. It might be time for us to admit that our lunches resemble a refueling manoeuvre more than a proper meal—you know, the aerial refuelling manoeuvre that you see in military documentaries—as you grab, chew, swallow, and type all at the same time.

Wellness ritual #1 is very simple: Revamp food selection to fuel your success. It starts with the belief that your daily eating habits are critical to fuelling your body with nutrient-rich foods to maximize your body's performance so that your body can in turn maximize your mind's performance. It is enacted with every food choice—fruits, vegetables, proteins, and water during every refuel.

Wellness Ritual #2: Exercise

I know you already know the benefits of exercise. Medical experts have linked regular physical activity with reducing stress, improving the immune system, and even slowing the process of aging. Chris Crowley and Dr. Henry Lodge, in their book Younger Next Year, drive this point home by differentiating between aging and decay, they state: "Aging is inevitable but decay is optional. The key to overriding your body's decay code is daily exercise." [3]

Why we should exercise should be pretty clear to everyone at this point. Many busy professionals, however, get stuck in the how, specifically, how do I consistently make time for it, given my busy schedule?

Being active is a natural inclination. Watch most children under the age of 10, and you will see them incorporate physical activity into everything they do. They run and jump just for fun. Conversely, take a look at the vast number of products marketed to adults that are designed to reduce physical activity— which is seen as a benefit.

Today we no longer need to move in order to work, shop, answer the phone, or even have meetings with people—so perhaps we need a new incentive to move. That incentive, I propose, is to increase your vitality and success.

Since this aspect is obvious to most people, I want to point out the obstacle that I hear most of my clients share (when they have fallen out of an exercise regime): Their biggest barrier is that they believe they don't have time.

It's not true.

If you are not physically active, it is not because of time; exercise is something that can be added to almost any activity:

- Stand-up desks
- Walking meetings
- Riding your bike to work
- Playing flag football with your kids or colleagues

I find that the relationship people have with moving their body is more correlated with the priority they place on themselves than with actual time constraints.

If you believe that you have no time to exercise, it's because you have a time scarcity mentality. I don't fault you for it though; many of us do. Since this scarcity mentality will plague you in so many aspects of your life that it's worth taking the time now to reflect on it and bust the myth.

Committing to exercise might just be the place to practise overcoming that thinking.

Busting the Time Scarcity Myth

As I pulled into the client parking lot (a little pressed for time), I was mentally reviewing the packed day ahead of me. First a team meeting, then an important client update, and finally a new project launch in the afternoon—there was a lot to fit in—so I knew that I was going to have to skip my workout.

That's when my cell phone rang.

My son needed stitches and was on the way to the hospital. In an instant, my priorities shifted. Just a few minutes before, I would have sworn I didn't have any extra time that day, but here I was, finding creative solutions for my commitments to get it all done. I did get it all done, and I carved out over two hours to focus entirely on my son before I was back at work.

I still skipped my workout that day, but the experience proved something important to me. When it came to an emergency, the claim that I didn't have time to exercise was simply false.

This emergency made me recognize that it is my prioritization and the value I put on an activity that drive how I spend my time.

On that day, it was the high priority I placed on being with my son that motivated me to alter my approach to meet my commitments.

It also showed me that my intense focus when I returned to work enabled me to complete activities much more efficiently than I would have otherwise.

Scarcity is the belief that there's not enough of something to go around.

Scarcity is an unhelpful mindset because it causes us to defend and hoard. Abundance, on the other hand, is the belief that "there's plenty and enough to spare", which opens us up to finding ways to make it all possible.

If you are not finding time for exercise, then I suspect you're not finding time for many other important and nurturing activities in your life either.

Here are a few tricks to changing your time scarcity thinking habit:

1. <u>Remind yourself that there are 1,440 minutes in your day:</u> When you realize that there are almost 1,500 minutes in a day, it's hard to believe that you can't carve out sixty minutes for a top priority. Don't buy into the always-in-a-hurry and never-have-enough-time culture; instead, say this sentence often: "I always have time for my top priorities."

Then ask yourself what sane living species wouldn't consider their vitality as a top priority.

2 <u>Ask yourself "how", not "if"</u>: When making decisions about your day, ask yourself "how" you can incorporate physical activity into your day, not "if" you can. See constraints as opportunities. When faced with a challenging constraint, turn it into a fun game—treating a deadline like a playful race against time. Model that attitude, and you'll be surprised at how quickly optimism becomes your default mechanism. Incorporate even the smallest amount of exercise daily, and be proud of what you were able to achieve.

3 <u>Value and appreciate the time you take for yourself</u>: A simple statement of gratitude before taking the time to exercise is "I'm grateful for this time and a body that is able to exercise. I feel fortunate to be able to care for my physical needs today." Use this gratitude statement to better transition into the activity so that you can enjoy it.

Exercise is a long-term play. The benefits of exercise can be subtle when you are in good health but dramatic when you are not. Your survival and wellness are critical to your success. Don't struggle with the small daily investment required; it is worth the gratification of a long and healthy life.

Finally, don't forget that this is easy and anything counts; wellness ritual #2 requires only that you choose to be active and move every day. It starts with setting your physical vitality as a priority and jumping at every opportunity to move.

Wellness Ritual #3: Sleep

How did you sleep last night? Did you get to bed late, making it hard to get up this morning? Or did you effortlessly spring out of bed feeling refreshed?

Know this—your sleep quality and quantity correlate over time with how well your days will go.

Inherently, we all know we feel better after a good night's sleep, but the actual function of sleep was not well understood until recently. Adding to the confusion, there seemed to be a lot of confusing role models—highly successful people who routinely burnt the midnight oil and bragged about it, as if it was a core competency and critical to their success. Personally, I love sleep— it is one of my favourite things—but I admit that I tried to hide my early bedtime from my workaholic management consulting colleagues. It was not cool to request a good night's sleep the night before a big pitch, although I do believe there would be a correlation with win rates if anyone would have studied it.

Thanks to Ariana Huffington and the many sleep experts that contributed to her book: *The Sleep Revolution*[4], we now know that during sleep many mental and physical restoration processes occur. These processes are critical for optimum performance, hence the third wellness ritual is sleeping an average of seven to nine hours per night. While you are sleeping, here's what you'll be doing:

Physical restoration:

- Repairing and renewing tissues and nerve cells
- Restoring the chemicals throughout your body and returning them to normal levels
- Healing your wounds and building your white blood cell levels, which provide your body's main defence against infection.

Mental restoration:

- Releasing stress-related neurochemicals like cortisol, adrenaline, and noradrenaline. The chemicals that were called upon throughout your day to enable your reactions to threats will now return to normal.

The release of stress-related neurochemicals is particularly important for professionals. The threat-related neurochemistry designed for confronting physical threats gets triggered throughout your day by intellectual or emotional threats.

These neurochemicals are released in your body to respond brilliantly to a physical threat. The body instantly receives more blood flow, energy, and strength. To accomplish this, it borrows energy from your immune system, your memory functions, your emotional regulation, and even your digestion. Since your body was primarily designed to move, run, or physically fight the threat, it is it is harder for your body to reset in the absence of this physical activity. Physical threats are also generally resolved quickly, whereas an intellectual threat can remain for days, weeks, or months. This is why sleep is so important for professionals; it provides a daily opportunity for your body to release your daily stress cocktail in times of prolonged professional stress periods.

Even naps can rebalance your neurochemistry and enable your mind to repair and restore over a short period of time, but you need deep sleep as well. Deep REM sleep completes important memory processing and learning, hence wellness ritual #3, sleep seven to nine hours per night.

Wellness Ritual #4: Stillness

So far we have concluded that you need to eat, move, and sleep—not rocket science, I know—but we are not done yet. Of all the wellness rituals that I urge you to master, this one I have found faces the most resistance.

Remember that all the wellness rituals, regardless of how common sense they are now, have faced opposition in their time. Scientists have challenged the criticality of nutrition and the effectiveness of exercise and Thomas Edison famously suggested that sleep was unnecessary. He even employed watchers to force his employees to stay awake all night until they got used to it (which they never did).[5]

Stillness, an ancient practice of consciously slowing down and clearing the mind's thoughts, is now becoming more mainstream because of its undeniable benefits. It's now abundantly clear that your mind benefits from stillness as much as your body benefits from exercise.

In the absence of a stillness practice, over time, your mind gets cluttered. Its performance deteriorates because it becomes wholly reactive. A stillness practice helps maintain space for fresh thinking. A mind that is trained with a stillness practice is able to process information in the moment with much less reactivity, such that there is capacity for foresight.

Simply put, without a stillness practice, your mind gets out of shape. It no longer reserves space for thinking. Like a house inhabited by a hoarder, your head gets filled up with thoughts completely generated from your past experiences. As a result, you simply repeat old habits, statements, stories, and thoughts— all in an automated and reactive way.

As a child, when your mind was less full, you were filled with curiosity and openness to the world. This is what space does. Where there is space, we are naturally inclined to explore and find interesting things to put in the space. The space creates a pull.

As your life unfolds, you easily accumulate joyful and painful experiences that make an imprint on you. The painful experiences make you more vigilant and the joyful ones create attachment to your past choices. The result is that you can become much less curious and more sceptical of new experiences.

This eroding curiosity is damaging enough, but because our brains naturally bend towards survival instincts, the increased vigilance is even more crippling. In an attempt to protect us from future pain, everything starts to look like a threat. Even our accomplishments and achievements become a source of anxiety as we become more afraid to lose them than we are actually able to enjoy them.

This erodes our courage to make any changes, in an attempt to avoid future pain, failure, or loss. We also absorb more external fears, compounding our own pain as we appropriate much of the bad news our society imprints on us.

The good news is that this state of mind is easily rectified with a stillness practice.

A simple and routine stillness practice can help you maintain your youthful optimism throughout your entire lifetime.

You may already have a stillness practice that you enjoy. Here are the characteristics that I have found to be the most important for applying to our professional lives:

1 Deliberately reduce reactivity: For a period of time (2 to 45 minutes daily), practise being still and internally present, able to ignore noises and external distractions and diminishing fluctuating thoughts.

2 Create and imprint an intention: Choose, repeat, and imprint your greatest aspirations for yourself. Hold a deep sense of faith and trust in the state you desire. Maintain confidence throughout your practice that your aspirations are already unfolding.

3 Experience inner fullness: During your practice, allow yourself to tap into a sense of inner peace and fulfillment. With each breath, try to deepen that sensation. Focus on the tranquility that comes from within and that wants for nothing—hold and enjoy this state.

Any stillness practice that meets these criteria will yield results. It can be combined with movement, music, scents, and environments that support the experience. Here are some examples of stillness practices:

- Seated meditation
- Guided meditations or music meditations
- Moving meditations like yoga or tai chi
- Deep breathing exercises
- Time in nature
- Prayer

Use Your Stillness Practice for your Success

To unlock your unprecedented professional success, you are very likely going to need to make changes. By now, you may already have a list of some of the habits that you know are getting in your way but that you believe are hard to change.

This is where your stillness practice is a game changer.

If you've struggled with making a change in your life, you already understand that your daily actions and behaviours are not always those of your choosing. Some of your own thoughts or behaviours just seem to happen to you rather than you choosing them. The reason for this is that much of your thinking is fully automated, powered by your unconscious mind with underlying assumptions that have formed beliefs.

Think of beliefs as the way your mind generalizes, organizes, and automates your responses. Beliefs are important for efficiency; they enable quick reflexes and energy optimization for your mind. These beliefs are formed by your past thoughts, emotions, and experiences. Your mind then uses them to guide your future.

Remember, your mind is mostly automated and unconscious. Estimates by physicist Maicon Santiago put the average human brain processing power at around 400 billion bits of information per second. The conscious brain (what you are aware of) processes a fraction of this at 2,000 bits per second.[6] That puts your maximum conscious absorption at less than 0.000001% of the information available to you. It is therefore your unconscious thinking (patterned by your past) that filters and creates rules for decision making via beliefs and habits.

This is important for our cognitive processing because without these filters, the information coming at us would overwhelm us, but it also creates a significant bias in our thinking that cannot be ignored. Thankfully, this programming is not static; it is formed and reformed throughout our lives, but because it biases our thinking, it tends to reinforce itself since we often don't even stop to consider our choices anymore. We conclude automatically without any thought, further reinforcing the historic pattern.

This is what makes change more difficult—the automation of the old belief, not whether you can be different, just whether you mindfully repeat the new behaviour or belief enough times to yourself for you to become different.

There is only one way the brain automates, and that is through repetition. Since the repetition of a new belief is unlikely to come from your current environment, you need to create it—in your daily life or even simply by creating the repetition in your stillness practice.

For you to understand the transformational power of shifting your beliefs, you have to experience it for yourself. I have found that a great way to experience this is to first identify a sticky belief that you know you want to change.

A sticky belief is a deeply seated belief that's semi-unconscious. It's semi-unconscious because you recognize it every once in a while and become conscious of not liking it, and yet it still continues to pop up occasionally. It can be a low-risk belief that you doubt influences your behaviour significantly but that you would still like to change. Don't worry about how you got the belief; what's most important is that you realize that it has become unhelpful and that you want to change it.

My Sticky Belief

After working for large enterprises for my entire career, I developed this sticky belief:

> *"Working for a large enterprise provides stability and resources. Running my own business is financially risky and harder."*

I cannot specifically trace what led to forming this belief, but I knew it was there, because I would catch myself thinking that running my own business was risky and hard. My brain was also very quick to show me lots of people who had an "inferior" quality of life to mine who had chosen an entrepreneurial path. Conversely, my brain was much less efficient at coming up with counter examples.

Despite the fact that I was doing well financially, I realized that my aspirations for my business were likely unconsciously limited by this belief. I realized that the belief was not helpful for many reasons, including the following:

1. I'd chosen to start my own business.
2. I was loving my work and working for myself.
3. I was making good money and growing exponentially.
4. The belief made me think small. It didn't bring me energy, ideas, enthusiasm, or growth opportunities. It simply stalled my progress and success.

So it had to go!

How I Used My Stillness Practice to Overcome It

To change this limiting belief, I simply needed to relax my mind and mindfully tackle the belief. The mind knows only repetition. It absorbs best when it is relaxed and unpressured. It will memorize your new belief simply by hearing it over and over again and by visualizing the wonderful impacts and emotions that the new belief makes possible.

I created self-guided meditations for myself that I listened to every day. I chose self-guided audio meditations because I find this form of meditation the easiest. It is also very effective, in fact a study at Harvard surprised the medical community when the results showed that participants' gray-matter density increased in a mere 8 weeks with daily practice. [7] Our gray-matter density is important for learning and memory functions - who doesn't want more of that?

Sure enough within a few weeks of listening to my meditations, my new beliefs took shape. I now feel that running my own business is more financially rewarding and less risky since I'm at the helm of it and I'm going to make it happen. I feel lighter without the burden of that old belief.

Interestingly, I also started to remember obvious but buried facts that I had completely forgotten, specifically that my mom was an entrepreneur, and so were my grandfather, great-grandfather, uncles, aunts, cousins...My new belief formed on its own naturally. It became "It's easy for me to run and grow my own business because it's in my blood!"

I understand if you think this seems strange—I was reluctant too. You just need to experience it to believe it.

I have now created hundreds of personalized meditations for my clients (only those who feel open to it), and all of them report positive impacts from listening to them. They experience firsthand the power of imprinting their own thought patterns through guided meditations. Some of them have used them to repair challenging relationships, increase their confidence, become more open minded, or even endure and triumph over cancer treatment.

My suggestion is that you embrace this and add it into your routine. Pick out a semi-conscious pattern that may be holding you back. Then pick up a pen and become the author of your desired beliefs—the ones designed for you that only you know. Create your own mantras specifically written to replace the unhelpful thoughts, one by one.

Here are some examples of mindset shifts that my clients decided that they wanted to change (consider, as outlined below: moving from ... to more ...)

Moving from... to ...

Cynicism to **Positivity**	Pleaser to **Co-creator**
Competition to **Collaboration**	Individualist to **Common good**
Survival to **Prosperity**	Controlling to **Inspiring**
Insecurity to **Confidence**	Knowing to **Listening**
Fear-based to **Faith-based**	Protecting to **Sharing**
Isolation to **Belonging**	Recognition to **Contribution**
Judgemental to **Curious**	Scarcity to **Abundance**
Reactive to **Proactive**	Frustration to **Openness**
Busyness to **Purposeful**	Constraints to **Possibilities**

Once you have identified the belief you would like to change, you can use the following template to build your affirmations. This will provide you with content for a 10-15 meditation, ideally recorded in your own voice and set to relaxing meditation music. Listen or read your affirmations once per day—and effortlessly transform your thoughts. You can also try the Work Smart daily meditation by going to **www.leaderley.com/WorkSmartMeditation**

AFFIRMATION TEMPLATE

Opening:
Every sunrise marks a new beginning. At the start of this new day, I take the opportunity to commit to my intentions. I breathe into this new beginning.

GRATITUDE:

I am so happy and grateful for the fact that ....

....

I am so fortunate to consistently find myself in the right place to

....

I appreciate and welcome the challenges I am facing so that I can become

....

RELEASING:

I now release any negative thoughts, feelings, or associations with ....

.... that I realize could hold me back.

I am willing and able to leave .... where it belongs, in the past.

I reject any limitations, and I believe fully in ....

BELIEFS – Releasing Fear:

I relax fully as I ....

I always find comfort and the help I need no matter how bad things seem

when I ....

Each and every day I feel more relaxed knowing I am ....

BELIEFS – Facilitating Change:

I feel ...., and these positive feelings naturally propel me forward.

Ten years in the future, I can see myself as a role model and an important

member of society. This makes me feel so ....

I feel a sense of joy and pride as I see my future self ....

....

BELIEFS – Stimulating Transformation:

I find ways to ....

I fully believe that I am ....

I feel confident that I can ....

BELIEFS – Reconnecting and Balancing Relationships:

I see my relationships with people improve and deepen as I ....

I feel connected and supported by others as I ....

Others are always available to me and I receive all the ....

.... I require.

BELIEFS – Solving Problems:

It feels wonderful to be guided by my inner sense of ....

It is easy for me to resolve ....

It is easy for me to accept challenging situations since I ....

BELIEFS – Strengthening Intuition:

I see myself celebrating my achievement of my goals with ....

I have trust in ....

I have absolute certainty that ....

BELIEFS – Relaxing into Your Perfect State:

I have all the power within me to ....

I am smart enough, good enough, and committed to ....

I am willing to be who I need to be to ....

MOTIVATING FEELINGS:

I am filled with excitement and energy as I ....

It feels amazing to fully believe in my abilities and my future, and I am so grateful for ....

I smile when I realize how ....

COMMITMENT and ACTIONS:

Even though at times I am uncomfortable, I am ....

I am willing to do whatever it takes to ....

I am now ready to ....

Closing:

Today I will focus my attention, energy, and efforts on the things that will yield the highest return. Being present and moving towards my goals feels so great. I breathe, and I grow.

Integrating wellness ritual #4 into your daily life will continually refresh and renew your thinking. This will create the space necessary for unlocking new layers of success that are critical to working smart.

Wellness Ritual #5: Human Connection

The final wellness ritual is human connection.

I don't have to tell you that you are human, but the implication of being a human should not be lost on you. In contrast to many species, humans are wired to connect to each other.

Let's take the example of our friend the freshwater turtle. When it is time for the mommy turtle to have a baby, she climbs out of the water, finds a patch of dirt or sand, digs a hole, lays her egg, buries the egg, returns to the water, and swims away. When the baby turtle hatches, it breaks open its own egg, digs its way out of the deep hole—sometimes for as long as seven days—then makes its way to the water's edge and swims away to find something to eat. The mommy and the baby turtle NEVER meet.

Contrast this with your early days as a human—unable to eat, move, or even burp on your own. Human survival depends on being socially connected. Primates are among the most socially connected species, and humans are more socially connected than other primates. As a human, you are wired for social connection and experience real suffering when you don't get enough of it.

Physical proximity is only part of the story. Despite the fact that we have greater population density and are more digitally connected than we have ever been, modern life is making us lonelier. This is not good news, since recent studies reveal that loneliness has been linked to a 26% increase in mortality risk in humans. [8]

That's because social pain is real pain; fMRIs (functional magnetic resonance images) of the brain confirm that the same areas of the brain are stimulated for social pain as are stimulated for physical pain. Chronic pain, either physical or emotional, can limit our ability to do our best work. In fact, emotional pain is said to have a greater negative impact (lasting longer and ultimately causing more damage [9]) to our professional lives.

Research confirms that our fundamental need for daily human connection is as basic as our need for food and water. Furthermore, lack of social ties has also been linked to cognitive decline in studies conducted by Harvard Medical School. [10]

The importance of the need and benefits of human connection is underestimated by many corporations and employers. While all organizations deliberately incentivize people with pay and perks, intrinsic motivators like social praise, compassion, thoughtfulness, and ensuring an environment free from social threats get less attention.

To become unstoppable professionally, you will want to develop meaningful relationships and genuinely engage in conversations with people that you care about every single day.

Unplug to Connect

Despite living in a highly connected world, growing evidence suggests that a sense of disconnection (and isolation) is linked to higher consumption of social media and communications through digital connections. Not only are we spending more and more time on our devices but our devices are also polluting the time we do have with each other. A series of studies from the University of Essex Department of Psychology actually revealed that the mere presence of a smartphone in the room negatively affected how people were able to relate to each other in conversation. [11] Try spending a little less time with your devices and you may find that your sense of human connection, wellness ritual #5 improves as well.

There you have it, competency number 1:   Be well.
Enhance your commitment to your wellness rituals, and it will pay off in your performance.

"Do You See Yourself? You're Glowing!"

I was at a networking event and ran into some old colleagues of mine. One by one, they shared with me how great I looked and asked me what my secret was. (One person asked if I was having an affair, of all things.) I laughed and kept saying the same thing: "It's no secret. I just got my wellness rituals down: I'm eating well, exercising, sleeping, meditating, and genuinely enjoying the interactions with my clients and colleagues more than ever before."

I guess it just showed.

COACHING EXERCISE

WELLNESS RITUALS
For each wellness ritual, indicate your current performance.

Healthy Food: ◯ Needs work ◯ About right

Exercise: ◯ Needs work ◯ About right

Sleep: ◯ Needs work ◯ About right

Stillness: ◯ Needs work ◯ About right

Human Connection: ◯ Needs work ◯ About right

Priority declaration–identify the area to work on first:

Decide and Do. Commit to an important item: ....

....

The Why. State the desired positive outcome: ....

....

The Reward. I will gift myself this reward: ....

....

EMPOWERING BELIEFS
Check off the beliefs you have right now (notice the ones you may want):

◯ I'm destined for greatness.

◯ There are abundant opportunities.

◯ Success is inevitable.

◯ There are many paths.

◯ I have many helpers.

◯ I'm uniquely skilled.

◯ Failing to act is the only failure.

◯ Self-expression is my birthright.

◯ I always have time for my top priorities.

◯ I'm grateful for every step on the journey.

◯ ....

◯ ....

NOTES

W	WELL
O	**OPPORTUNITY-ORIENTED**
R	RELATIONSHIP-DRIVEN
K	KIND

S	SUCCESSFUL
M	MANAGERIAL
A	ACTION-ORIENTED
R	RESILIENT
T	TENACIOUS

O

OPPORTUNITY-ORIENTED

Seeing Opportunities— Always and Everywhere

"How can you be so positive?" I'm sure many of you have asked someone this question before. I get asked this pretty frequently myself, and yet when I'm feeling down while others are maintaining a positive outlook, it still impresses me.

Where does the ability to remain positive and see opportunities come from? Well, the technical answer is your prefrontal cortex.

Your prefrontal cortex is the part of your brain located right behind your forehead. This area of your brain is the youngest (evolutionarily speaking) and the most advanced. It is responsible for your highest and most complex cognitive thinking.

Most importantly, it is where your imagination lives.

Your imagination is the place where you generate foresight, make predictions, and evaluate potential outcomes—the place where anything is possible, where you are naturally biased towards your success. You can engage it right now by simply asking yourself, "How might I make this possible?"

There are other parts of your brain, though, whose job it is to balance out this optimism, downregulating it with fear and pessimism so that you don't put yourself at risk.

Understanding the dynamics of all of these brain networks is extremely complicated and is not yet fully understood by scientists. Nevertheless, the functional models that have been developed already have proven useful to my clients and have helped them to become aware of their thinking habits and skilled at knowing where their thinking (and others' thinking) is coming from—as in, which part of the brain.

I have found that as my clients build their brain awareness, they learn how to tap into their highest cognitive capabilities in the moment and unlock self-management capabilities on a whole new scale.

To give you this super power too, I first need to give you a sense of the dynamics at work between your ears.

Here is a quick run-through of your four functional brain networks that drive your decision making and opportunity orientation.

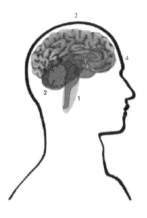

From oldest to youngest:

1. Reptilian brain

2. Mammalian brain

3. Neocortex

4. Prefrontal cortex

Meet your reptilian brain: The reptilian brain is the oldest and most primitive part of our brains. It is responsible for consolidating information from our senses and looking for threats. This part of the brain is hardwired to protect us from harm to our body or ego. It is always looking for perceived danger and working to protect us. The reptilian brain has the ability to shut down our thinking and unilaterally decide how we react. When this brain is alerted to a threat, our behaviours are limited to the following:

- **Fight:** Argue, attack, or block
- **Flight:** Reject and mobilize to avoid
- **Freeze:** Hide and protect
- **Appease:** Acquiesce, pander, or surrender

Meet your mammalian brain: The mammalian brain is also known as the emotional part of our brains. This is where our emotional experiences are accessed. This part of the brain is wired to help us nurture and build relationships. It reads the social context, scans for inclusion or rejection, and provides us with our emotional experience of interacting with others, both good and bad. The emotional brain also regulates and recruits the other areas of the brain based on its observations. For example, when the emotional part of the brain identifies a threat, generally in the form of rejection or exclusion, it will hijack our thinking by summoning the reptilian brain to react. The emotional part of the brain also creates a sense of emotional safety when it deems we are in a trusted environment. In this case, it engages the prefrontal cortex directly by urging it to take action to shape more of this emotionally fulfilling experience into our future.

Meet your neocortex: The neocortex is often referred to as the rational part of our brains. For professionals, this area of the brain is our workhorse. It performs much of our thinking and reasoning and houses our language and cognitive skills. It maintains our procedures and frequently accessed memories. When the reptilian brain and mammalian brain are relatively content (meaning they do not feel threatened), the neocortex operates well. The only real threat to this area of the brain is overwhelm, when our prefrontal cortex does not give it sufficient direction or prioritization. The reptilian or mammalian brains, of course, can prohibit it from focusing whenever a threat surfaces.

Meet your prefrontal cortex: Now you have reached the summit—your prefrontal cortex, where your highest-level coordination of the whole brain occurs. This area of the brain envisions the future and has the ability to connect with others with compassion and build deep trust. Most importantly though, this is the only part of the brain that is able to deal with uncertainty. You want to spend as much time as possible activating this part of your brain, but to do so, you have to keep your reptilian and mammalian brains happy. As long as they are happy, the only thing that could limit activity in this part of your brain is if you choose to spend insufficient time reflecting on your interests. Your prefrontal cortex wants to engage and help you with your highest aspirations. It is therefore important to spend time figuring out what those are. Once you do, you will have a partner in working to achieve them.

Now that you know their technical definitions, I want to help you understand how to manage their interplay. To do this, I find it helpful to give them some nicknames.

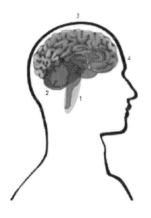

Brain Nicknames:

1. Your Chief Risk Officer
2. Your Chief Relationship Officer
3. Your Chief Operating Officer
4. Your Chief Executive Officer

Obviously we all want to be taking direction from our CEO, but as all CEOs know, input from the other executives is important too. No CEO that I know, however, who will allow important decisions to be made unilaterally by their chief risk officer. That's why the CEO's vision needs to be clear and compelling for all of these important stakeholders. *So how do you align all of these parts of the brain to support you?* You have to tell them a good story.

This is because the stories you tell (to yourself privately) orient your thinking.

Our stories about our professional experiences are particularly critical to activating our minds. Specifically, maintaining an opportunity orientation to everything and anything that we experience requires that we have a compelling story that unites all parts of our brains.

A Sample Story to Deconstruct Together

We were walking out of a train wreck of a meeting. Our proposal pitch did not resonate with the Vice President of Finance. Our solution was focused on optimizing the company's global talent distribution and operating model. His focus and questions were all about the risks of the change and how we expected to mitigate them. Insufficiently prepared for this line of questioning, we were extremely deficient and lacking in our responses to his concerns. This did not reassure him at all, and he basically shut down the meeting, saying just that. Then he sent us off to do our homework.

I felt humiliated and really angry at myself. My head hung down as we walked. When I finally looked up, my colleague, an amazingly talented leader, was just smiling and said, "Now this is going to sharpen our thinking—how exciting!"

Let's break this down in brain terms:

- Our pitch was focused on our vision for the future organization, a conversation geared at the prefrontal cortex.
- Because our proposal insufficiently accounted for the risks to the organization and employees, the VP's thoughts became dominated by his emotional and reptilian brain.
- With his brain in this state of reactivity, he did not have access to his prefrontal cortex to envision the opportunity.
- The VP's reaction then triggered my emotional and reptilian brain as I felt defensive and rejected.
- My colleague, on the other hand, was able to maintain his prefrontal cortex activity; he was visualizing the opportunity for a positive future outcome.

Stories that Activate your Prefrontal Cortex

Since we don't have a remote control to turn off or on certain areas of our brains, we need a different approach for orienting our thinking. This approach is simple but deliberate. It involves mastering five storytelling rituals that you can use to maintain your mind at its highest thinking, and you will use these five opportunity orientations to navigate even the most difficult of situations:

1. Success is probable.
2. There are multiple chances and many paths.
3. The journey is rewarding and interesting.
4. Failing to act is the only failure.
5. This work is meaningful.

Opportunity Orientation #1: Success Is Probable

Just like most Hollywood movies, very successful people practise the art of Happy Ending Fabrication in their internal storytelling. They practise a mindset that actively and deliberately fabricates happy endings and holds them in sight at all times.

They maintain an unrelenting faith that a successful outcome is in their destiny.

As alluded to earlier, this is not a natural state of mind for most adults. Some of my clients immediately reject the suggestion to embrace their optimism, claiming that their fear drives them to prepare better or come up with more complete answers. Neurologically, though, this is proven to be false.

Our minds gravitate to either fear or faith. You end up in one or the other.

If you are skeptical about all this positivity and believe that you perform better under pressure, I recommend you read the book, *Performing Under Pressure*. [12] This book puts to rest the idea that people perform better under pressure. The evidence points to the opposite: Pressure reduces our performance.

This is because the fear state activates the reptilian brain (our Chief Risk Officer) creating tension and in turn triggering defensiveness and protection instincts. Just like at the end of the meeting with the VP of Finance, when I was definitely in my reptilian brain because:

- I wanted to hide.
- I didn't want to face the team to tell them how it went.
- I wanted to defend the quality of our existing solution.
- I was even shaping my rebuttals to the VP's criticism.

Every thought was reactive. My precious and brilliant neurons were not firing in my prefrontal cortex. I was stuck in negative stories with no faith (the belief that a positive outcome is probable) in sight.

When my clients share their dramatic tales in vivid detail of the untenable situations they are facing, I have deep compassion for them. I get that it is not always an easy practice to maintain the belief that a positive outcome is probable. It's sometimes difficult to even see success as possible, let alone probable.

I say probable because if I claim it's guaranteed, I rightly might just get thrown out of their office. My experience is that success is virtually guaranteed when leaders are able to embody optimism and faith because this mindset allows them to generate and collect the exact ideas and approaches that lead to success.

Unlike the chicken or the egg riddle, there is no riddle here—the faith comes first, and the solutions follow. Your faith is required so that you are able to access your prefrontal cortex and your highest cognitive abilities to figure things out.

Opportunity Orientation #2: There are Multiple Chances and Many Paths

This opportunity orientation emphasizes that you have many chances to address any challenge and that there are many paths to success—innumerable paths in fact.

The "work hard" mindset will fight this position. It will insist it is right with statements like:

- "You might have already blown it."
- "You only have one shot at this."
- "You better get this one right—or else!"

It is damaging to put these unnecessary and unhelpful limitations on the human mind. They only serve to intensify our negative stress, reduce our intelligence, and strip out any fun in our lives.

It is also quite irrational. There are very few situations in life where we only get one shot. Our lives are lived in a continuum of experiences and decisions that ultimately support everything that we achieve. They don't always come when we want them to, which can cause frustration, but that's a trap too.

If we allow ourselves to get caught up in every discrete frustration instead of just seeing it as a step in the journey, we become tired.

Choosing a path is the antidote for uncertainty.

Standing at the edge of a very dense forest, unsure of how to navigate through it, will naturally create uncertainty. And yet by activating our prefrontal cortex accesses our "knowing", the awareness that we are headed in the right direction (even if detours are likely) and makes us confident that we will get to where we are going. This is the certainty we require to be successful since it opens up our capacity, creativity, and resolve to endure and even enjoy the journey.

This is a skill especially relevant today, with many people navigating multiple career changes, employers or pursuing freelancing opportunities. These dynamic careers can create uncertainty or enable endless possibilities, when you remain opportunity-oriented.

Opportunity Orientation #3: See Problems as Interesting Opportunities

Stories are enhanced with a few surprises. No one likes a story without a few plot twists.

Our careers inevitably have texture to them as well.

This is why I encourage my clients to think of their problems as plot twists that add richness to a good story. Problems that arise are matched with solutions and open up insights that streamline our processes.

Maintaining an opportunity-orientation while facing daily problems requires special stories. The way we shape our problem solving stories and rituals influences our cultures. Personally, I have observed three common mistakes leaders make that lend themselves to less opportunity- oriented cultures:

1. Creating a Hero Culture (overreliance on individuals)
2. Creating a Root Cause Culture (overemphasizing causation)
3. Creating a Catastrophizing Culture (exaggerating problems)

The Hero Culture

The good thing about a hero culture is that these organizations reward and value their most talented problem solvers. Generally, these heroes are well-known, well-treated, and celebrated. The downside of this culture is that maintaining your hero status depends on having lots of problems and differentiating yourself as other people's saviour. This can have the effect of allowing systemic problems or process issues to endure since the heroes always swoop in to save the day. An organization that relies on specific individuals to perpetually solve problems instead of developing leaders that coach and involve all team members to continuously improve processes will ultimately suffer inferior performance.

The Root Cause Culture

On perhaps the opposite side of the scale is a root cause culture, where much of the attention of problem solving is centered on deep analysis of the problems to eliminate them. Data is meticulously reviewed and events are reconstructed in an attempt to pinpoint the exact sequence of events that led to the problem. Then top talent is tasked with prevention and never letting the problem happen again. Of course, this is a good thing, but with so much effort expended on analysis and mistake prevention, much less energy is given to creation and the innovation cycle that depends on iterations and even some unexpected surprises.

The Catastrophizing Culture

There are also catastrophizing cultures, which are often created by jittery leaders. A catastrophizing culture exaggerates problems and makes them appear bigger and more systemic than the actual problem at hand. This is sometimes deliberately orchestrated in order to stimulate a sense of urgency or to justify a change, but over time, it erodes effectiveness and invites complacency. Since employees eventually grow tired of the agitated state, it hinders the organization's ability to accomplish anything as it veers from one perceived catastrophe to another. Escalating emotions, excessive worrying, and lots of false diagnosis is bad for the human brain.

What's a WORK SMART problem-solving culture?

A WORK SMART culture remains opportunity-oriented above all else. This means that leaders are focused on what the problem enables versus how the problem will be solved or avoided in the future. This starts with acceptance and then viewing the problem as neutrally as possible: "A problem is neither good nor bad; it is an opportunity to learn."

Many leaders fear this approach, they worry that seeing problems more neutrally will lead to complacency, but I see it differently. The hero culture, root cause culture and catastrophizing cultures anchor our thinking in the past. Opportunity-oriented leaders are future-focused thus seeing problems as critical to designing a better future. When embraced as an opportunity to improve, mistakes and problems transform into an intricate optimization loop that leads to greater success.

Carla Ruben, Owner and Founder of Creative Edge Parties, recognized the importance of getting the right problem-solving culture embedded in her company. It was, in her view, critical to delivering on the brand promise. Creative Edge Parties' promise is to deliver unparalleled culinary experiences combined with immersive design, spectacular aesthetics, service and event execution excellence. Getting the details right, means everything for her business. In any given event, even though hundreds of details are perfect, there are often a dozen that could have gone better. How to remain intense about those details without demoralizing the team and minimizing their accomplishments? A WORK SMART culture, one that is able to celebrate accomplishments while identifying opportunities for even more precision in the future. The trick is to not make anyone feel blamed, to see the problems more neutrally, and review the information to guide the team to:

1. See issues as objectively and as neutrally as possible (identifying all attributes as either positive ones or less so)

2. Seek many views to understand the original intentions and actions that make up the context of the situation

3. Brainstorm options for next steps or revised approaches that are directionally correct (even if imperfect)

4. Take action and monitor progress to capture all new "information" from the next iteration

This approach to facing challenges and obstacles keeps our rational and executive brains engaged and avoids triggering our reactivity.

Opportunity Orientation #4: Failing to Act Is the Only Failure

The meaning you give to your failures and mistakes is the most important story you craft.

As a coach, I pride myself on being skilled at helping my clients unlock their untapped potential. I really do think of it as unlocking because the capability is already there; it's just not accessible to them. What I help them do is find the key.

The key that unlocks this potential usually requires transforming a fear that they hold privately into an opportunity. The fear they are holding is very real and was formed for a very rational reason. It was formed based on evidence and logic during real and tangible experiences. Strongly-held beliefs are usually lessons learned anchored from our past experiences from previous successes or failures.

These "lessons" teach us to avoid repeated failures and help us to repeat successes, which is useful, but they can also be insufficiently precise for our current challenges and limit us from experimenting with new approaches.

Limitations most often spring from our desire to avoid failure.

That is why our storytelling and re-storytelling about the lessons learned from our mistakes and failures are so critical. The trick here is to continue to revisit the lesson and sharpen it. If you do not reframe the failure, when this fear is triggered, your emotional brain will regenerate all of the past pain, and you will re-experience this pain and reactivity, thus blocking your creative thinking.

One of my clients was increasingly frustrated with the unrelenting lack of alignment in his team. He felt very strongly that they were smart individuals who should be able to collaborate. He was an extremely talented and engaging communicator with a very diplomatic conversation style.

He had been rewarded in his career for this communication style that he had mastered at a very young age because his father had a very bad temper; he learned how to communicate to avoid escalating it. His style was therefore very measured and warm, so it was always very pleasurable to talk to him.

When I met with the members of his team, I began to understand the potential problem. His team members shared that each of them, in their one-on-one discussions, would individually consult with him on their mandates. They would seek his direction, and they would leave the discussion believing that they had his full support.

Then they would begin executing and run into all kinds of misalignments because their initiatives were at odds with their colleagues' mandates.

The communication style that this leader had developed during his childhood contributed to a lack of clarity in these one-on-one meetings. The reason he was not more assertive or direct was because he unconsciously avoided conflict.

When he realized that he was operating from the more primitive area of his brain (avoidance), he was able to envision a new outcome, one that had a positive outcome for everyone. He could provide clear direction to his team by facing conflicting points directly and supporting their facilitation once he engaged the COO and CEO areas of his brain.

With the highest areas of his brain activated, this leader was able to shift his communication style to a much more transparent one and transform the outcome for him and his team.

Opportunity Orientation #5: Generate Meaning for Your Work

The stories we tell ourselves about the work we do either make our work harder or easier. Or said another way, the stories we tell ourselves either give us access to our entire intellect or only a small percentage of it.

The storytelling ritual of determining the meaning in your work puts you on a course to bias your daily activities in support of that meaning. Meaning is fuel for your prefrontal cortex, and the more you create meaning, the more energy you will have for your highest level of thinking.

Therefore, Job #1 = Creating Meaning

When I sense that my clients are working far too hard, I can just feel that they are running low on meaning. We run low on meaning when the CEO of our brain is dormant. When the stories in our heads are all about reacting to external demands, we lose our sense of purpose, and this exhausts us over time.

The most interesting part is that the activity that we are working on may very well be meaningful to us, but unless we engage our prefrontal cortex with this meaning, it will not feel that way. The good news is that the experience of the task can be completely transformed by deliberately engaging our higher-level thinking and identifying the meaning in it.

Meaning is also personal. For some people, the simple motivation of winning, producing, or selling something provides sufficient initial incentive to support their efforts. It is important to realize, however, that without the engagement of your prefrontal cortex, over time most activities and financial rewards will be insufficient to maintain your full motivation.

To consistently inspire your best work, you want to engage your CEO brain to become a meaning-manufacturer. You can do this by identifying all of the collateral benefits that will result from the task at hand. Things like: Personal growth, enjoying others, quality output, impact, beauty, or creative self-expression.

Smart, opportunity-oriented leaders understand the power of engaging their higher-level thinking through their storytelling so that they can endlessly replenish themselves instantly and effortlessly. In any task where you find yourself calling on your discipline to push through, realize that you are missing a key ingredient: add meaning through story.

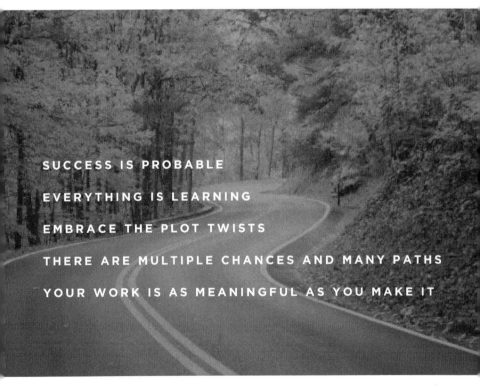

SUCCESS IS PROBABLE

EVERYTHING IS LEARNING

EMBRACE THE PLOT TWISTS

THERE ARE MULTIPLE CHANCES AND MANY PATHS

YOUR WORK IS AS MEANINGFUL AS YOU MAKE IT

Now that you have all the storytelling rituals you need to remain opportunity oriented, it is time for you to engage the CEO of your mind to become the author of your own life. If you are resisting this chapter, your emotional brain is likely presenting you with some counterproof, arguing that storytelling is fantasy and futile.

It may even pull out a deeply painful past experience to illustrate to you that no amount of storytelling would have avoided the situation you were forced to face. You may feel defeated and reject the opportunity to take hold of your own pen. This is another fear—because you are worried that your writing will be vandalized by another author, that life will keep throwing you obstacles that you would never put into your script.

I get this. None of us are the sole authors of our story. There is a co-writer called life that from time to time sneaks experiences into our storylines. Still, as long as you allow your emotional brain to extrapolate from the past rather than harnessing the power of your prefrontal cortex to drive opportunities for you, you will feel stuck.

Your stories have more power than you think. They transform your experience of living and literally open up or shut down your brain's intellectual abilities.

Don't let your primitive brain run the show. Decide to be opportunity oriented in every moment.

COACHING EXERCISE

BRAIN AWARENESS

Identify a recent experience that triggered the primitive areas of your brain (reptilian or mammalian)

Now think of an equally challenging situation where you were able to remain in your higher-level brain (neocortex or prefrontal cortex).

WHAT DID YOU DO DIFFERENTLY?

Identify the stories and thoughts that enabled you to maintain higher cognitive intelligence, in the latter experience:

The vision was

The intention was

The meaning was

The plan was

The support was

NOTES

W WELL

O OPPORTUNITY-ORIENTED

R RELATIONSHIP-DRIVEN

K KIND

S SUCCESSFUL

M MANAGERIAL

A ACTION-ORIENTED

R RESILIENT

T TENACIOUS

R

RELATIONSHIP-
DRIVEN

Success is amplified by quality relationships

I don't know how many times I have heard the following words uttered in business: "You don't need to like them, but you need to work with them." Now, I do not blame you if you are among the many that have accepted this unfortunate belief. I do, however, urge you to abandon it. If you would like to be successful beyond your wildest dreams with ease and joy, you will replace this belief. Instead, I want you to say, "My success is directly correlated with my ability to weave quality relationships with as many people as possible."

Working smart requires others. Plain and simple, you have no chance of achieving the success you desire on your own. No chance. Period.

This means prioritizing relationship development over task execution.

If you are like me—a highly driven, ambitious, productive person who likes to get things done—you may be allergic to this statement. But it's still true.

That's because you probably envision yourself—with deadlines looming—having to waste immeasurable amounts of time and faking interest while listening to stories about other people's pets, children, or hobbies. You will be happy to hear that this is not what I'm asking of you.

You can walk and chew gum at the same time, and you can also enhance every working relationship in parallel with completing your deliverables. If, however, you focus only on the deliverables and the deadlines, you will damage relationships, which will hinder both the quality of your outputs and the trajectory of your career.

To be relationship-driven means to be consciously aware of your impact on everyone you work with. It means proactively creating environments where people can collaborate to do their best work. It means taking it upon yourself to develop others even when it is not in your direct interest, leaving them better than you found them.

Once you agree that this is a real priority for you, there is one major blind spot that you should be aware of: Your self-awareness will have you evaluating your performance based on your intentions. The problem is, when it comes to relationships, *others-awareness* is far more important than self-awareness. This is because your relationship outcomes will be solely driven by the impact you have on others, regardless of your intention.

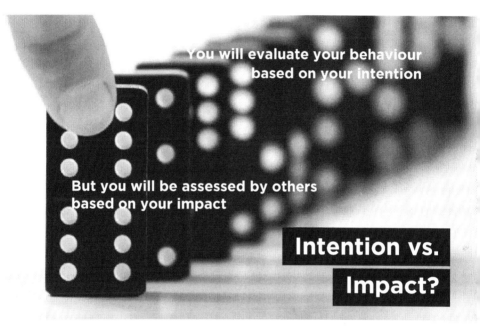

You will evaluate your behaviour based on your intention

But you will be assessed by others based on your impact

Intention vs. Impact?

This may feel similar to another frustrating truth that all professionals need to deal with, the infamous "perception is reality". I suppose this is a version of that truth. Regardless of your intention, if the impact on the other person was negative, you are guilty of causing that negativity.

In order to guide you into the transformational experience of transitioning from ME focused to WE focused, there are five important relationship-building tips to build your competencies:

1 Learn to de-escalate
2 See potential in everyone
3 Always tell the truth
4 Practise being level blind
5 Co-create instead of influence

Relationship-Driven Tip #1: Learn to De-escalate

This first relationship-driven tip relates to applying your CEO mindset (your prefrontal cortex) in support of elevating others who have become highly reactive facing a challenging moment. Relationship-driven leaders are able to manage their own fears and refrain from engaging in unhelpful dialogue or actions in the moment.

For me, this is like an oath of non-harming and recognizing that when someone is overly stressed, aggravated, unprepared, or failing to manage their time, it does not help for me to dramatize it. This does not mean that I ignore or minimize the gravity of the situation. Many times I'm co-dependent on their success, so of course it creates anxiety for me as my mind visualizes all of the negative implications for my own needs. It does mean, however, that I choose my words and actions carefully, such that I support them in stabilizing and mobilizing them for the best outcome possible.

In other words, I help them access their higher level thinking.

To accomplish this, the smart leader focuses on de-escalation and temporarily drops the content, long enough to stabilize the individual's reptilian and mammalian brains. You don't put gas on the fire; you help to put out the fire by showing curiosity, under-standing, empathy and offering to help.

WATER	GAS
Curiosity	Disinterest
Understanding	Defensiveness
Empathy	Apathy
Help	Blame

This requires that you focus on better understanding the situation, remain supportive, and offer your assistance even if you disapprove of the behaviour.

Don't get me wrong; it is a natural instinct to blame, show disinterest, or act defensively, but your discipline to overcome this temptation comes from your determination to maintain or improve every relationship in every interaction.

I also think it helps to remember that their behaviour is not who they are. Their aggression is caused by their own suffering. You might be the receiver of the aggression but it has very little to do with you. This is why if you allow them to externalize their pain (remembering that their aggression is a call for help) you can be much more efficient and focused on their real need. This means choosing compassion for their externalized suffering, rather than mirroring their bad behaviour back by becoming defensive or aggressive yourself. Supporting their de-escalation with dignity and respect is your investment in the relationship. It will pay off. Making your future collaborations easier and easier.

De-escalating Versus Appeasing

A little side note for clarity: Some of my clients, when I discuss the deliberate use of this de-escalation technique, confuse this advice with being asked to pander or appease their aggressors rather than push back and defend themselves. I want to be clear that de-escalating should not feel this way. Appeasing is a stress response that we may well use when we are feeling overpowered; it is a tactic that we use to survive an aggression by being submissive so that the perpetrator stops and we escape and survive. This is not what I am advocating here. De-escalating is an empowering and deliberate response to support the individual and, over time, will have a positive impact on their behaviour. This is not about agreeing with the behaviour, only about impacting them to improve it in the most effective way. De-escalation should feel empowering and energizing.

Relationship-Driven Tip #2: See Potential in Everyone

Being relationship-driven requires that we see the potential in others. It involves helping them stretch themselves while holding aspirations for them in the process. It also means that we encourage their authentic voice even when we are afraid of what they are going to say, because it is part of their development process.

It helps me to think of everyone as bru-tiful! As this word implies, we are both beautiful and brutal, but we are all more beautiful than we are brutal (at least 62.5% beautiful, if you count the letters). Relationship-driven leaders see the beauty in everyone while considering the brutal as beauty in development.

"Origin: A mix between the word Brutal and the word Beautiful. Coined by underground death metal/comedy band Masked Penguin Slaughters."

I am brutal and I am beautiful. You are beautiful and you are brutal.

The beautiful part of me includes my current and expressed brilliance—the refined beauty that is present in my thoughts, words, and actions. My brutal part—the unrefined, struggling, and resistant aspects of myself—is still very much in development.

Relationship-driven leaders see the relationship struggles and conflict as potential for greatness. The beauty is making its way down its own kind of birthing canal—painful and bloody yet necessary and joyful.

Growth requires support through resistance. Relationship-driven leaders know when to pressure test, but they don't push too hard. They understand when the individual's real need is to be held higher and bigger than their behaviours or even how they see themselves. Seeing potential means you hold space for others to grow into, you support their aspirations, and you hold your mind focused on the other side of the struggle.

As a relationship-driven leader, you imagine and foreshadow their next level of potential unfolding in front of your eyes.

Relationship-Driven Tip #3: Always Tell the Truth

By the time I come to work with my clients to support them in working through challenging relationships, it is very common that there has been very little truth-telling for quite some time.

The spokes on the relationship wheels are horribly bent after months of conversations severely lacking in transparency.

When you hold back your truth by sharing incomplete or false information, you are bending the spokes on your relationship wheel, and from there, it gets very wobbly.

People come by these truth-telling transgressions honestly. They are trying to avoid demotivating or hurting people, so they elect to keep their true feelings to themselves. The problem is, our feelings are impossible to contain within ourselves. Our activated feelings fuse into every facet of our being, making them somewhat difficult to interpret but transparent to others in very confusing ways. We become awkward and seem inauthentic and untrustworthy, which plagues even the simplest of communications.

The relationship is riding on a very bent wheel.

The solution to righting the relationship is always straightening out these spokes by getting comfortable with proactively sharing our feelings and observations in a way that is respectful and that does not make the other person feel wrong. Sharing the impact a situation is having on you is not the same thing as accusing others of causing this impact on you.

When a child accidentally knocks over a glass of water, the ice cold water on your lap could make you jump and react, but it is easy to comprehend that the child did not intend to cause you harm. The same is true of every professional transgression.

It is through transparent dialogue that leaders are able to reconcile intent versus impact.

The simple format for this conversation is as follows:

"This 'event' caused this impact, which made me feel this 'feeling'. Can you help me understand your thinking or intention?"

Having these conversations early and often bolster both alignment and trust. This is done by anchoring in our shared humanity outside of any structural hierarchy. We begin by assuming that the other person had a positive intent. We are then transparent about our sensitivity and the impact they had on us. Through this open dialogue we build a shared understanding of each other's viewpoints which eases future conversations.

The best test of your truth-telling is to simply hold yourself to the following standard:

1. If I am persistently thinking about it, then I need to express it to them directly.

2. To express it to them and have a positive impact, I need to refine it.

3. If I won't refine it and share it, I refuse to think it.

This simple test will encourage you to plan and have truthful conversations. Having these conversations will relieve you of the burden of carrying volatile thoughts around with you every day. When you force yourself to clean up your thoughts and to consistently have transparent conversations, you feel so much more stable and confident in your engagement with others. What we don't always realize is that carrying volatile and unrefined thoughts takes a lot of energy. We live in a constantly controlled state to prevent these thoughts from sneaking out. Rightfully so, because they are in fact waiting for a weak moment to escape—a moment where an external situation triggers their outbreak.

To be clear, I don't want you to hide your thoughts. I want you to refine them and share them openly in a way that creates a positive impact and maintains full integrity in your thoughts and words.

Relationship-Driven Tip #4: Be Respectful while Ignoring Hierarchy

Most of my early memories of my parents entertaining guests involved my dad bringing very senior leaders from Ford Motor Company over to our house for dinner. My dad was in his mid- to late thirties and on the fast track, being promoted to more senior leadership positions and already in the succession plans for the C-Suite. For my part, this meant that I had to dress up for dinner that we would eat in the dining room, that I would need to be polite, and that I would likely be bored out of my mind.

As a five-year-old I honestly thought that these so-called leaders were just normal people, who were a bit obsessed with their work. They could talk about nothing else because all they thought about was their job. I found these conversations extremely repetitive and dull.

I didn't realize until many years later what an incredible gift this was. Being subjected to these early experiences meant that when I entered the workforce, it never occurred to me to be intimidated by anyone due to their so-called position. This meant that I could be myself and do my best work without all of the nerves that many of my peers were experiencing when they were exposed to the most senior leaders.

These jitters are super unhelpful and completely unnecessary since kindergarteners would run circles around these same leaders.

It is extremely important for your ease at work that you be confident with all of your colleagues, and this includes feeling like a peer to the C-Suite. This confidence comes from focusing on how much you are the same.

I can't count the number of times I have heard from senior leaders that in order to fully support my client in progressing to the next level, they would like to "feel like they were a peer". That's it. They have all the competencies, but there is hesitation about their readiness because they don't feel like the other person feels ready.

When I bring this feedback back to my clients, I'm always a little worried that they may find this to be too vague to act on. But they almost always agree. They say, "They're right. I don't feel like a peer."

The obvious fix is to elevate yourself by seeing your sameness. When you tap into your sameness, your confidence swells.

Think about all you have in common:

- You are both humans, leaders, teammates
- You are both good at what you do
- You both strive to add value
- You both have information you would like to share

Tactically, all you have to do is the following:

- Recognize when you subconsciously feel less than a peer.
- When you meet with them, sit closer, and make more eye contact.
- Consciously focus and notice your similarities.
- Proactively ignore any differences or status symbols, seeing these as simply small variants and preferences.

Or pretend that you are in kindergarten and try to imagine how boring you might find them.

Don't forget that this also applies to your direct reports—you want the same from them. You want them to feel comfortable sharing their best ideas and expanding their contributions. You can accelerate this by helping them to feel like your peer because we are peers—we're all humans. When we focus on our shared humanity rather than our hierarchy and differences, everything gets easier.

Relationship-Driven Tip #5: Co-create instead of Debate

A common goal of many of my clients is to improve their ability to influence others. Influence is, of course, important in our professional lives and critical to our success. We have goals and objectives that require resources, and we need buy-in from others to achieve our objectives. There are inevitably others that may have structurally conflicting roles or incentives that can conflict with our own. In order to be successful in these contexts, we need to develop influencing skills.

Here's the paradox: I have yet to have a client come to me asking me to help them improve their openness to being influenced by others, and yet our influence on others is correlated with our openness to being influenced.

The easy path to influencing and attracting followership lies in our co-creation skills.

Whether we acknowledge it or not, we are all co-creators of each other's experiences with our daily interactions impacting each other.

If we seek to interact with someone simply to influence them without being influenced ourselves, we enter the interaction focused on our position. This will cause us to hone our senses and receptors towards our rigid positions and look for ways to overrule their position. This suboptimal state is damaging as it causes both individuals to take on rigid, robotic, inauthentic, and forceful stances. Worse than that, it simply invites resistance as the other person's protection instincts kick in since we are most definitely triggering each other's primitive brains.

The result is that we further diminish any influence we may have had by allowing the conversation to resemble a winner-takes-all battle.

This is completely unnecessary since the real key to influencing other people is being open to allowing them to shape you. You gain influence when you give influence. I have seen this time and time again. Co-creation trumps influencing skills.

My client Dany Hebert, the IT change management lead for a global SAP implementation, called me one evening right after she applied this approach. She was so excited and happy she couldn't contain herself. Dany had been in a power struggle with her boss over a decision to move forward with a consulting vendor to source talent for an important role. Her boss didn't want her to proceed with her preferred choice and she had been advocating and trying to convince him for several weeks.

I told her to build three options and to detail out the benefits and risks of each option but to include only options that she could live with. Then I suggested she go to him, explain the options, and ask him for his suggestions to sharpen her analysis. After she took his input, I suggested she ask him to pick the supplier—simply hand over the reins and give him the chance to make a unilateral decision. Of course, she didn't like this suggestion at first; it was her budget, her accountability, and her problem if she didn't get the work done - so she wanted to make the decision herself.

As an experiment, she followed my instructions and reviewed the options with her boss. He made some slight modifications, and then she specifically said, "These all look doable, and I'm comfortable I can make any of these work. What would you prefer?" To her surprise, her boss said, "Well, what is your preference?" and proceeded to allow her to choose. She couldn't believe it and was elated. She got her choice, and by relinquishing her position, she earned his trust and was able to proceed with her preferred vendor.

What is the moral of the story? Co-create, give your power away, and it will be handed right back to you. Allow others to shape you, and you will shape them.

Now it is your turn to start relentless relationship building.

Being relationship-driven means striving for the highest-quality professional relationships with everyone you work with. It means using every opportunity to enhance that relationship.

It means valuing others and fighting the tendency to make others wrong. It requires releasing our desire to be right and recognizing that to succeed we need others and to build advocacy in others we need to embrace their preferences and ideas.

It involves soliciting the right kind of engagement from others and encouraging them to augment your ideas rather than tear them down. It means considering many viable paths and continuously shaping and refining those paths with each other.

It doesn't mean you always have to agree, but it does mean that you always need to be in integrity and be transparent. It isn't hard. There is nothing easier than being authentic and honest—it is the real you, and it's magic!

COACHING EXERCISE

KEY RELATIONSHIPS
Identify a key relationship in your professional life, and consider the following 2x2 matrix [13]. Determine which quadrant your current relationship resides in.

Now consider bringing that relationship to the Co-Creating quadrant. Which actions will you take to start?

Increase alignment:

- Solving for each other's metrics
- Understanding each other's constraints
- Actively finding synergies
- Advocating for each other's success
- Publicly acknowledging & supporting each other's growth

Increase influence:

- Providing access to useful information
- Developing and sharing your desirable expertise
- Holding influence with key individuals
- Being recognized as a leader within the group
- Creating mutually beneficial wins

NOTES

W WELL

O OPPORTUNITY-ORIENTED

R RELATIONSHIP-DRIVEN

K KIND

S SUCCESSFUL

M MANAGERIAL

A ACTION-ORIENTED

R RESILIENT

T TENACIOUS

KIND

Creating a positive work environment

Sometimes I find it useful to notice how much of our business terminology originated from military combat. Even very commonly used words like strategy, tactic, campaign, alliance, collaboration, and recruitment originate in war. Add to this all of the sports analogies: the ball's in their court (tennis), keep your eye on the ball (baseball), down to the wire (horse racing), the gloves are off (hockey), drop the ball (football), or slam dunk (basketball). It's no wonder that our professional lives can feel like an arena.

These terms were all designed to elicit obedience and compliance to rules. They puff up our competitive spirit (a win–lose mentality) and narrow our thinking while depersonalizing our opponents. Perhaps you could argue that this is useful in getting work done in a rules-based context; however, it isn't great at generating ideas, building solid relationships, or co-creating solutions.

With these power plays swirling around us, it is no wonder that we feel anything but inclined to be kind. Kindness has little relevance in most "games" as individual interests swell, making us internally focused if not totally selfish.

And yet the ease that comes with an altogether different approach, one that leads to higher levels of success, is rooted in kindness. You being attentive and in service to others' needs.

The effectiveness gain that you achieve when you adopt a kinder and more generous approach to work is impressive and sometimes very surprising.

One of the reasons your effectiveness will climb so dramatically is because you will be able to tap into greater intelligence, the intelligence known as collective intelligence. That is the collective intelligence of all of your collaborators.

One interesting study at Harvard [14] demonstrated that individual intelligence is easily trumped by collective intelligence in business. This group intelligence also had little correlation with the intelligence of its members. The study found that the teams that demonstrated the highest performance together were able to do so because of other characteristics (unrelated to their intelligence scores). The characteristics most observed were that the teams listened better to each other, shared feedback constructively, and were open minded. In other words, they were kinder.

In this chapter, to get tactical about being kinder, we will cover the following:

1. Expand your objectives to accommodate others
2. Improve your listening skills
3. Build deep trust
4. Show appreciation, and provide useful feedback
5. Pay attention to your own reflection
6. Practice gratitude

Kindness Tip #1: Expand Your Objectives to Accommodate Others

I think it is useful to think about kindness on a spectrum, with low kindness being defined as the absence of consideration of others (or selfishness).

Unkind = Ignoring negative impacts on others

The way we tangibly start being kinder is by expanding our focus to include others in our own projection of success. I find it important to define how we do this because kindness cannot be faked. Kindness is felt—specifically, felt by others—based on whether they perceive that we have their best interests in mind.

Many of my clients are skeptical about whether being kind is really necessary in business. They really don't believe that it drives effectiveness gains. Before they try it, they need to believe in it enough to even recognize it. I give them this hint about what to look for.

The efficiency gain that most of my clients see when they begin to behave in a kinder manner is primarily in the implementation phase of all of their collaborations. When they apply more consideration of others, this usually requires that they have more discussions and more listening up front, which can make people feel like they are spending more time accommodating others. So if you look for gains in this phase, you will most certainly be disappointed. The performance gains of these practices instead come during implementation—where the payoff is. Going too fast during alignment by excluding others' ideas or needs can feel faster but ultimately creates more expensive execution challenges, more difficult change management, and less effective solutions.

And accommodating others doesn't need to take that long.

As a tool for my clients in preparing to accommodate more kindness (defined as consideration of others), I suggest that they remember and practise the very simple exercise of reflecting on others' perspectives even before they meet with them. This activity primes them for more social awareness even before the group meeting. The more self-reflection there is on others' agendas, the more their thoughts and behaviours will open up to accommodate others' needs. I often remind them that people's agendas are not so complex. Everyone has the same one: They are trying to maximize their gains and minimize their losses, so it's not rocket science to figure out each other's needs.

EVERYONE WANTS THE SAME THING

MAXIMIZE GAINS

MINIMIZE LOSSES

The exercise I recommend for priming our minds for collaboration is to grab a piece of paper, draw a box for each person, and scribble down the following:

YOU	THEM (NAME)	THEM (NAME)
Perceived Gains	Perceived Gains	Perceived Gains
•	•	•
•	•	•
•	•	•
Potential Losses	Potential Losses	Potential Losses
•	•	•
•	•	•
•	•	•

For the specific initiative you are working on, you can very quickly see others' perspectives and find ways to adjust your own objectives to accommodate as many of their needs as possible. Don't worry if you don't have all the answers yet as to how to do this. That's what the group's intelligence is for. Your job is simply to be open and accepting of their needs.

Kindness Tip #2: Improve Your Listening Skills

Now, as you prepare to meet with your collaborators to tap into your collective intelligence, I need to warn you about something. Your listening skills are probably pretty bad. I say this because we are all pretty bad at listening. We all have bad listening habits.

These are partly due to our design. Our brains, for the sake of efficiency, are extremely biased, and therefore our thoughts bias our listening. Remember, your mind is a filter and an organizer. It is always trying to decide what is important in order to log the information in a logical "spot" attached to something that it already knows. This means that we are always presuming that what we are hearing is similar to something we already know, because that's the easy path for logging the information. If what we hear is really different than what we know, it takes much more energy for our brain to process. That's why we have to pause when we hear something completely new—because our brains literally have to create a new neuropathway, and we aren't sure where to put this new information.

This takes energy, and because we have evolved to be energy efficient, we fight the tendency to want to absorb a new thought. If we are really tired or overwhelmed, we fight this a lot, preferring to become impatient with each other when the conversation is not lining up with what we were expecting to hear.

Overcoming this inertia by improving your listening, though, is necessary for you to build effective collaborations. Not being listened to is one of the most painful human experiences, and it is extremely unkind.

The first step to improving your listening is figuring out your predominant listening habit. It might resemble one of these ways of listening:

- Identify a problem in order to provide a solution
- Assess whether we agree or disagree
- Uncover risks and implications
- Find weaknesses in the rationale
- Avoid being influenced by the individual altogether
- Find an opportunity to jump in and share our ideas

These are common listening contaminants because they all turn our attention to our own thoughts as we iterate through our own determinations. The more we are thinking, the more we are:

① assuming we understand;

② planning our response; or

③ judging the content or the individual.

Having a lot of thoughts swirling around in your head makes your listening a "side job", thereby blocking your comprehension.

Physiologically, your own thinking blocks your ability to form mirror neurons, which are fundamental to maximizing your collective intelligence. What is a mirror neuron? Mirror neurons are special to primate species. They are specific neurons that fire and "mirror" the behaviour of another person as though you yourself (the observer) were experiencing it yourself. An article in Harvard Business Review summarized the importance of mirror neurons like this:

> These neurons create an instant sense of shared experience.
> This allows individual minds to become, in a sense, fused
> into a single system. We believe that great leaders are those
> whose behavior powerfully leverages the system of brain
> interconnectedness.[15]

Not only is listening kind but it also helps top leaders increase their effectiveness by tapping into the collective intelligence of their teams.

Here are the steps to practically apply to deepen your listening and increase the activation of your mirror neurons.

STEP 1: Listen for feelings only.

Inquire and share openly how everyone is feeling in the moment or about the situation. Talk about it until your feelings seem in sync and stabilized on common ground in the right frame of mind to begin the discussion.

STEP 2: Listen to connect to their experience.

Withhold your judgement about the content or its relevance to you; instead, keep your focus on connecting to their experiences. Avoid linking it to yours; just see yourself in their story.

STEP 3: Now listen to understand.

Now, with your mirror neurons firing, you are ready to understand the content. Focus on absorbing their understanding. Ask questions to bridge any gaps between your realities and theirs. Stay in this dialogue until everyone can see the world from their eyes.

Step 4: Listen for opportunities for mutual success.

You will find that any attachment you may have had to your original opinions should have evaporated. You are now focused on creating something new together. This is where you design and create plans to strive for mutual success together.

Step 5: Listen to close any interpretation gaps.

Reveal your insights and replay your interpretations to confirm and sharpen your shared understanding. Celebrate the achievements of the dialogue. Forgive each other for any clumsy moments.

Kindness Tip #3: Build Deep Trust

One of the common barriers to our ability to be kind is an unconscious lack of trust. Neurologists are beginning to understand that this "trust switch" seems to be caused by a part of the brain called the temporoparietal junction (TPJ). This area of the brain (that sits at the intersection of the emotional brain, the neocortex and the prefrontal cortex) has a very important function. The TPJ integrates information both from the external environment and from within the body. It processes it to determine whether we will connect with the person. Specifically, it correlates with whether we will allow ourselves to feel empathy for the person. [16] In simple terms, if the TPJ deems that we can empathize with someone, then our neocortex and prefrontal cortex open up, and we begin to share openly with them. If it deems that they are "not like us" and we cannot relate to them, it shuts us down and sends us into the primitive brain.

This unconscious distrust switch is a real liability for us in the workplace since it can be triggered incorrectly, misinterpreting situations or blocking the connection to the individual simply because of their role or some kind of structural misalignment or perceived competition. Overcoming this involuntary response requires making conscious attempts to remain open and engaged in conversations in order to build rapport and build shared understanding.

When a client of mine resists accommodating another person's perspective and struggles to be kind, insisting that no win–win solutions are possible with them, it is most often due to their lack of trust and the flick of their TPJ. Once the TPJ is flipped, we begin operating in distrust, whether we intend to or not, to protect ourselves. This fear-based survival instinct causes us to be unkind in subtle but pervasive ways.

In her book, *Conversational Intelligence* [17] Judith Glaser describes how our behaviour changes in a fear-based response.

FEAR RESPONSE	INSTEAD OF
Exclude	Include
Judge	Appreciate
Control	Expand
Withhold	Share
Assume	Discuss
Dictate	Develop
Criticize	Celebrate

The very first step is to build your awareness—the critical awareness that helps you to catch yourself in these behaviours and realize that you are being limited by your primitive brain.

Once you recognize this, it is time to proactively reset the interaction to build trust.

You can use the adapted trust formula below from Conversational Intelligence® [17] - to support you in advancing trust:

T **Transparency:** Sharing what you honestly believe. Including who you are and what you think. This supports building trust, even if you fear that revealing yourself, weakens your position.

R **Reliability:** Ensuring that you consistently meet your commitments to others. If this becomes impossible, immediately apologize, re-promise and deliver on your revised commitment.

U **Understanding:** Stand-Under-Their-View; seeking understanding, making sure you release any judgement in order to see their unique perspective clearly.

S **Shared-Wins:** Finding ways to shape shared goals and intentions that are mutually beneficial and "safe" in that they sufficiently accommodate each other's needs.

T **Track-record:** Establishing a track-record of collaborating and achieving together. Having shared experiences where your integrity and commitment to each other was tested in action.

Remember to iterate through the framework as often as you need to, even within relationships that are strong, to sort out any misalignments that surface. Creating trust will create much more ease in your work.

Kindness Tip #4: Show Appreciation, and Provide Useful Feedback

Now that you understand why being kind is so critical to your success, you may be wondering what to do if the nature of the situation requires that you deliver unkind news. What if, for example, you need to deliver performance feedback and it's not going to sound kind?

Many people avoid giving proper feedback. When they notice behaviours that are damaging or inappropriate, they themselves experience physiological stress and try to find reasons to avoid discussing it. In general, I find the most common reason people are fearful is that they are unsure whether sharing their insights will even help. This is a reasonable fear since poorly delivered feedback can damage your relationship with the other person and even trigger defensive or retaliatory behaviours.

In fact, in a study published in the *Harvard Business Review*, the research team quantified the ideal ratio of critical to positive feedback and its impact on team performance.

The study found that teams performed at their best when the ratio remained below 1 criticism for every 5 positive comments. When the dosage climbed to 2 negative comments for every 3 positive comments, the cocktail was practically lethal to team performance. [18]

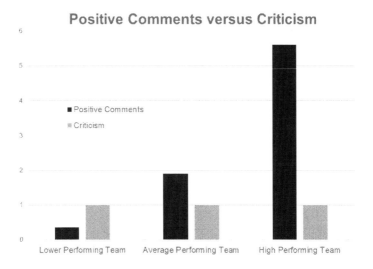

Positive Comments versus Criticism

This is not the only study that has demonstrated the potential negative impacts of critical feedback. There is growing evidence that criticism has an overall negative effect on performance.

The findings from this particular paper are enlightening in two ways. One insight is that we really do need to turn up the amount of positive feedback in the workplace since I am certain that the 5 to 1 ratio is unattainable without a deliberate increase in positive feedback. The second insight is that we also need to avoid criticism as much as we can because there's a good chance (even with expert delivery of the feedback) that your words may be interpreted as criticism even if you didn't mean them that way.

The recommendation here is therefore twofold: Leaders need to be more direct with positive feedback as well as more refined in how they deliver negative feedback in order to meet this negative-to-positive feedback ratio.

Here are some tactics to get you started:

1. Detailed appreciation
2. Future-oriented aspirational input
3. Co-created reflective feedback
4. Catching them doing it well

1. Detailed Appreciation

Many leaders are often vague or even subtle when it comes to delivering positive feedback. They imply that people did a good job rather than overtly telling them so. This is a mistake. Leaders should go out of their way to notice and appreciate excellent work and should be extremely specific, identifying the specific attribute that they think led to the job well done. Example: "Great work on that report. I could see how well you planned the milestones, managed the team's input, and demonstrated such great attention to detail. Your efforts created a very positive experience for everyone involved!"

Detailed feedback not only sounds more credible and is more likely to be absorbed but it also supports the individual in specifically identifying what they did well and therefore should repeat. Recognizing only that the report was good does not support them in recreating the next success as they may not have noticed themselves what led to the meaningful outcome.

Making time to notice and provide detailed appreciation to your teammates is critical to your success. Jim O'Connor, former Chairman and CEO of Ford Canada reinforced this point to me, he shared: "Each day I devoted my first 30 minutes to dictating short recognition messages to at least 20 employees or dealers. I must emphasize the importance of this: It is the leader's job to create the environment for success and appreciation is a big part of that."

2. Future-Oriented Aspirational Input

In this approach, the leader shares feedback in the form of aspirations for the individual such that they begin to see themselves bigger in their own future self.

For example, if you have an employee that struggles to share their opinions in a group, you could share this aspirational feedback with them: "I can't wait for the day when you routinely contribute in every team meeting so that everyone can benefit from your input as much as I do when I engage with you privately." Now you have seeded this possibility into their imagination. This will alter their behaviour more quickly than forcing them to contribute.

3. Co-Created Reflective Feedback

With co-created reflective feedback, you actually don't need to do very much talking at all. You simply facilitate the thinking. You ask them to share with you following an important activity by asking them two questions:

"What went well?"

"What could have been even better?"

In this reflective feedback approach, you let them go first, and you keep nudging them to add to their reflections. Most of the time they will self-identify the vast majority of observations that you would have said. When you ask them what could have gone even better, you will hear their ideas for growing and developing—all without you having to say a thing.

At the end, you can round out their feedback with any important items you feel they missed, but the less you say, the better; the more they create the input, the more motivated they will be to take action.

4. Catching Them Doing It Well

A final approach does not require you to deliver feedback at all. The process is to reflect on their development needs and then determine the opposite behaviours. Then you begin to look for those behaviours in other contexts. This requires intensely observing the individual until you catch them doing it well somewhere else.

Say, for example, you notice that one of your employees talks too much in the team meeting each week. Instead of telling them not to talk too much, make a mental note to notice their behaviour in other meetings. As soon as you see them listening and collaborating better, pull them aside and compliment them, saying, "I noticed that you were extremely respectful and interested in including everyone's opinion. It was exciting to see how other people really stepped up. Beautifully done!"

A few reinforcements like that and their behaviour will shift without using up a dose of criticism.

Now with these 4 great tactics, you will be able to shape most people's performance and develop the skills they require to prepare them for expanding opportunities. Don't forget to celebrate improvements publicly and keep development suggestions private.

But what if you are forced to make a change?

In your ascension to top leadership, despite your best efforts, there will likely be times when performance deficiencies, restructuring or cost optimizations will force you to make staffing changes. This decision is easier if someone lies, cheats or steals from the company. In that case you want to objectively share the facts and act decisively and quickly. It is more difficult, however, when workforce reductions are a result of cost optimizations, restructuring or performance issues. In these cases, almost everyone hates letting people go, but still has to do it. The process is painful for both the giver and the receiver of the news. The best advice I can give you (having let go of many people myself) is threefold: 1) do your best to avoid surprises, 2) be as generous as you can on transition support and 3) show-up with compassion, respect and appreciation for the individual.

To avoid surprises make sure you have foreshadowed the possibility and communicated it effectively. Giving people the chance to pre-process the change will ease the acceptance of the news. As much as possible, there should be no new information shared at this time. The economic or performance issues should be well known and the individual should have witnessed obvious attempts to avoid the situation. You can remind them of your efforts and appreciate theirs. Then offer the best transition support you can, remind them of their skills and capabilities and offer them encouragement. Regardless of their reaction, your responsibility is to remain respectful, compassionate and connected to your shared humanity.

These conversations are difficult, but the possibility for an amicable separation exists. If both parties understand the need for the change and are willing to take responsibility for themselves, they will be able to accept the decision even if that means agreeing to disagree. If you follow these three principles, you will be as kind as possible, under these difficult circumstances.

Kindness Tip #5: Embody the Behaviours you want to See in Others

As part of my most popular executive coaching program, we kick off in the first month by identifying a few of my client's key stakeholders. These are individuals who play a pivotal role in my client's success. I meet with each of them privately to better understand my client's unique strengths and also to drill down on what their leaders and team members want to see in order to fully support my client in progressing to the next level.

Before I meet with the stakeholders, I ask my client to tell me a little bit about the individual that I will be interviewing. One of my clients, shared this about his direct supervisor: "She is a very talented leader but can be overly-opinionated. I don't always feel comfortable sharing my ideas with her. I wouldn't consider her to be the best listener in the world."

Then I met with his leader and heard very similar feedback but through a slightly different lens: "He is very talented but I don't feel like he shares his ideas with me openly. In fact, I'm not sure he's the best listener, because I repeatedly ask for his input. I wish he would contribute to our executive meeting with more ease and comfort (and definitely without asking for permission)."

What never ceases to amaze me is that the feedback is almost always a mirror image of each other's feelings. What is lacking for one person is almost always lacking in the other.

When I press my clients to invest in the relationship and try to make a change, they almost always suggest that they cannot do it alone, (the old – it takes two to tango) - but they can. There is a delay, of course, for the reflection to come into sync, but one person can absolutely shift the relationship because ultimately it is a mirror image.

This particular client did just that. He shifted the relationship once he realized that he and his leader both had the same unmet need: To share their ideas and be heard. From that day on, when his leader shared her opinions, my client demonstrated his listening skills by playing back what he was hearing to confirm his understanding. This small shift dramatically reduced the amount of time his leader spent repeating and asserting her position. It also created more space for his ideas, and over time his leader began to routinely play back her understanding making my client feel heard.

Remember, your needs are their needs. Being kind to their needs will help you to meet your own needs.

Kindness Tip #6: Practise Gratitude

In my experience, practising gratitude is a deeply rewarding activity that many people forget to practise. When we feel grateful, we are naturally kinder.

In a professional context, I believe that the biggest threat to practising gratitude is getting caught up in a sense of entitlement. Entitlement, in all forms, kills gratitude.

Due to the commercial nature of our professional context, we can easily get lured into entitlement thinking. I believe that our feelings of entitlement start innocently enough, with taking pride in our work and in our contributions thus feeling deserving of our compensation. This can cause our expectations to begin to grow as we advocate for our performance, and we begin to get consumed by the process, forgetting to appreciate it and be grateful.

When you stop enjoying your rewards and simply see them as entitlements, you know you have stopped being grateful. Feeling entitled always backfires; it also weakens our chances of being recognized at all. Like a spoiled child demanding a gift, others feel less compelled to be generous since the combative nature of our entitlement mindset influences others to protect their share of the assets and to share only the minimum amount necessary to avert a threat.

You can be assertive, proud, grateful, and highly successful all at the same time.

Examine your assumptions

Sometimes when working with my clients, we discover "false assumptions" that are inadvertently holding them back. This is almost always a foreshadowing of a breakthrough for them. False assumptions are caused by accident as our minds link information together. This linking can sometimes get hardwired in our thinking, and we start believing we cannot be two things at the same time. It is similar to an overgeneralization. For example, "I only get my way when I'm assertive and angry." Now that this thought is linked in the mind, it may block us from being able to be assertive and compassionate at the same time. But once you realize that you have accidentally polarized two behaviours that could just as easily operate together, you can experiment with bringing them back together and rewiring your mind.

That is very often just the reboot you need—a fresh perspective that sheds new light on new models and new ways of being that will support you in reaching unprecedented levels of performance.

That is what happened to me regarding being kind at work.

With all the adrenaline, testosterone, and competitive spirit swirling around me, it was tempting to copy being tough and demanding to get things done, but it never felt good. Once I learned that I could be kind, grateful, and successful all at the same time, work got a whole lot easier.

COACHING EXERCISE

ACCOMMODATING OTHERS

Identifying mutual interest: Use the following section to identify perceived gains and losses for someone with whom you struggle to align.

You   **Them**

Perceived Gains: ....   Perceived Gains: ....

....

....

Perceived Losses: ....   Perceived Losses: ....

....

....

Identify a few mutually beneficial objectives: ....

BUILDING TRUST

Which fear-based reactions do you need to be more aware of, and which trust-based behaviours will you up-regulate?

Down-regulate fear: **Up-regulate trust:**

○ Exclude   ○ Include

○ Judge   ○ Appreciate

○ Control   ○ Expand

○ Withhold   ○ Share

○ Assume   ○ Discuss

○ Dictate   ○ Develop

○ Criticize   ○ Celebrate

Co-create feedback

What went well: ....

....

Even better if: ....

....

NOTES

W	WELL
O	OPPORTUNITY-ORIENTED
R	RELATIONSHIP-DRIVEN
K	KIND

S	SUCCESSFUL
M	MANAGERIAL
A	ACTION-ORIENTED
R	RESILIENT
T	TENACIOUS

S

SUCCESSFUL

Designing and Embodying Your Success

One of the most common traps that we humans, as social beings, are extremely susceptible to is borrowing our definition of success from others.

It can be borrowed from your parents or teachers or imprinted through socialization, trends, rebellion, or a desire for fame and fortune. We are so wired to seek out acceptance and recognition that we can be blinded from our own desires. Not to mention the fact that there are so many biased influencers taunting us and tempting us at every turn with big promises that lure us into their journeys.

Being thoughtful and authentic about your definition of success is critical to working smart. By this, I mean carefully reflecting on your desired objectives that adequately and meaningfully serve your interests and talents.

Success is not one thing.

Success is a concept that can only be appropriately represented when viewed as a complete system. It requires an examination of a number of vital components that make up your uniquely fulfilling life. The linkages and interactions between these components are as important as the individual components. It is honouring and working towards the entirety of the system that represents holistic success, considering all interdependencies. It is also not static and shifts over time, making it even more important to reflect, revisit, and reprioritize.

I like to use the following coaching exercise to help my clients illuminate their definition of success as well as identify areas where they can expand their success in a systematized way.

For this exercise, we draw a circle with approximately eight subsections and identify areas of our lives that are important to us. This list of items is unique to every individual but generally contains some of the following areas:

- Career
- Finances
- Family
- Friends
- Romance
- Learning

- Health
- Environment
- Exercise
- Recreation
- Mindfulness
- Adventure

Once you have identified your top areas, you dedicate a section of the wheel to each of the areas and use the wheel to score your current level of satisfaction in this area (on a scale of 1 to 10). Use the inner circles to denote the score.

Then draw the "shape" of your current success profile (see example below) and reflect on the top priority areas that you want to pay particular attention to. Circle the sections that you believe will contribute to uplifting the entire system.

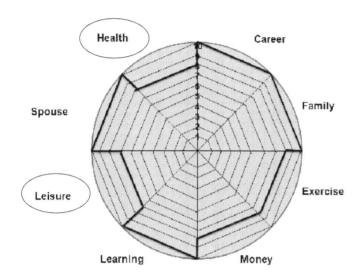

This quiet reflection is a good start to begin the inner listening required to set objectives that will guide you to your unique and balanced view of success.

Embodying Success

Success need not be viewed as a destination; it is a state of being as well as a guiding star that orients the actions you take. The biggest barrier to your success is the failure to fully embody it.

I recognize that this is a bizarre concept. It is one that I was particularly allergic to when I first heard it, but I have come to understand it and recognize its importance in addition to developing a few strategies for actually doing it.

Embodying our success is important because it is our best defense against the inevitable self-doubt that always gets stimulated when we begin to work and make progress towards our goals. In fact, sometimes our self-doubt and accompanying self-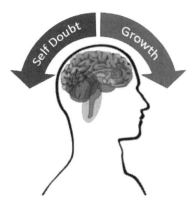 talk can get so noisy that even though we have earned the results we are achieving, we still feel like a fraud.

If we let our self-doubt overtake us, we start to hear questions like "Who do I think I am?" or "If they only knew how unprepared I am, they wouldn't..." These thoughts are simply not helpful; they only slow you down or stop you from fully engaging such that it will stunt the achievement of your dreams. Many people describe this as Impostor Syndrome.

First identified by clinical psychologists in 1978, it is officially described as "when high achieving individuals develop an inability to internalize their accomplishments and experience a persistent fear of being exposed." I suppose it is comforting that at least 70% of high achievers share in this tendency. [19] But it is a tremendous waste of talent, time, and energy. And its effects intensify, from anxiety, stress, and self-doubt to depression.

The key to overcoming this syndrome is to remove your dependency on external recognition and to strengthen your internal frame of reference and natural desire to grow. If you allow your success to be defined by external measures, the judgements of others will weigh heavily on you and always feel like a reward or threat. This is where the fear that others will discover you as a fraud comes from.

Embodying your success has nothing to do with any outsider's perspective on your performance. It is totally internally focused and focused on the success behaviours you are engaging in, not the outcomes.

Here are some examples of these success behaviours:

- Reaching for opportunities and learning
- Applying skills to the best of your ability to add value
- Trying to make a positive contribution
- Enjoying collaborative relationships

When you put your attention on the behaviours that ultimately drive your success and take action in them every day, you will notice that you are already successful even in this moment, right where you are.

Imposter or not, here I come

In preparation for writing this book, I researched, read and asked a number of published authors about their writing process. I picked up two pieces of advice that I found helpful: 1) Write daily and make it a habit and 2) Your biggest risk is not finishing your first complete draft so don't revisit anything until you finish it. These two tips became my measure of success throughout the process. When my mind attacked me with self-doubt (like you're not an author, you're a fraud) I would objectively look at my behaviours. Am I writing each day? Yes. Am I committed to finishing my first complete draft? Yes. Therefore, I'm already one of the most successful authors I know, based on the behaviours and actions I am taking. It is impossible to be found out as a fraud when you measure yourself against your success behaviours.

Align your behaviours and actions to your success definition and embody both your current and future successes. Your confidence will grow and the world will take notice.

Here are five success embodiment tricks to accelerate the process and deepen it further.

Success Embodiment Trick #1: Identity Shift

When I first started learning about the psychological importance of identity, I found it to be a bit of a foreign concept. To me, my identity was my name, my profession, my interests, and my family status. When asked to share my identifications, I would pull out my driver's license, not share a deep reflection.

To our minds, however, our identity (how we see ourselves) and what we identify with are critical factors in our behaviour. Our identity helps the mind organize and automate our behaviour. Hence, if you want to be more successful, you need to act more successful, and for you to do this much more quickly, you will want to first shift your identity.

Your identity is also private—just for you—like deciding you're a family person before you even have your own family. This is a decision to see yourself differently that subtly and pervasively shifts the way you behave, what you focus on, and your daily decisions and interests.

After you deliberately determine your own success definition, you will next want to figure out the implication on your identity and how your identity will need to shift to achieve the upgraded success profile.

In a professional context, say you are a very strong senior project manager and an expert at following methodologies and managing large teams, schedules, budgets, deliverables, milestones, and stakeholders, but you discover that you feel lacking in personal growth. Specifically, you want to bring more innovation and creativity to your work. In that moment, when you decide that you want to shift your identity from Senior Project Manager to Senior Innovation Lead, your behaviour can and will shift. As you walk into work the next day as Senior Innovation Lead, your experience of every meeting, every discussion, and every challenge changes because the lens you see it through has changed. Lo and behold, without telling anyone, you are engaging and enjoying your work in a brand new way.

My favourite example of this was brilliantly demonstrated by my former colleague Martine Lapointe. She shared with me her experience during her promotion process to Managing Director in Technology Consulting. She talked openly about how long and demanding the process was: "It felt like being under a microscope for over two years" she explained.

One morning, she realized that this scrutiny was distracting her from her work and her life - so she quietly decided to promote herself. She decided, in her own mind, that she would act as if she already had the role. She released any doubts and felt certain that the firm would eventually catch up. Of course, that year she did get promoted, since her behaviours followed her identity shift and ultimately accelerated the achievement of the milestone.

Your identity shift can be ambitious or even feel absurd to you when you initially conceive of it, but it is just the right size for you. Your desire to grow, create, and impact is the most effective navigation system for your career.

Success Embodiment Trick #2: Role Shape Shifter

One important obstacle that arises for people as they attune to their true and innate ambitions is how different these may be from their current reality. It is normal to experience tangents in our journey that may lead us further away from where we want to be.

If you notice that your current reality is pretty far away from your desired one, you may feel your life requires a major overhaul in order to achieve success as you have now defined it. This instinct for a fresh start then gets confronted with the practicality and obligations of your current context. The necessity for income, family obligations, and the reality of rattling your entire life ecosystem suddenly hits you. This can be very overwhelming and easily stop you from making any changes, especially when even your friends and family don't agree that anything is even broken.

This causes many people to give up on their success definition. Allowing their protection instincts to overtake them and deciding that things are "good enough" after all.

Others still will get so enthusiastic about their new destination that they will immediately begin to turn down or reject any opportunities that present themselves since they resemble their former journey, not their new thinking. These individuals make their path much harder by rejecting rich opportunities simply because they are worried the opportunity will keep them on their current path.

The smart approach is very different than these two common paths. It starts with full acceptance and appreciation for all of the experiences and assets accumulated on the current journey and revisits these to apply them to the new desires. With a revised view of success, the entire trajectory of the past needs a new look. The most obvious success story needs a rewrite based on a new end game. The reflection results in a new inventory of the past experiences and developed abilities that are most relevant to the new journey. These experiences and skills are in your past; they only need to be identified and brought into focus.

With this new perspective (a renewed appreciation for your experiences, skills and desired destination), it is now time to become a role shape shifter.

A shape shifter (a fictional character with the ability to change their physical form at will) has a super power that as a child, I really wanted. I loved the idea of transforming into a bird to fly and a fish to swim, perfectly adapting to the environment to suit my needs. Perhaps this is why I noticed this related professional phenomenon: role shape shifters.

The first Master Role Shape Shifter I encountered was a very talented leader named Bill Morris. I worked for Bill in my early 30s, many years before he became President of Accenture Canada. During those early days of working together I quickly noticed his accelerated career progression. He was being offered significant promotions with increasing responsibilities at an unmatched pace. Every time he accepted a new role, he would share with us the expectations and organizational impact. I remember it feeling like a bit of a goodbye since the new role would inevitably shift his focus. But no sooner had he accepted the role, he began to change it significantly—aligning it to his desires, figuring out ways for us to work together again, and restructuring such that he maintained responsibility for the most enjoyable aspects of his former role. He slowly shifted the role to precisely meet his own desires.

At the end of the two to three year assignment, the role he performed and excelled at was nothing like the role he had accepted and described in those first few days.

For a period of time, this pattern annoyed me. Why was he getting away with this? He had been hired to do one job, and he would turn around and do whatever he felt like—and he would be rewarded for it! The answer was super simple: He did his best work when he followed his desired path and his bosses appreciated the outcomes he was able to drive. I don't want to underestimate the skill involved. His approach not only accommodated for his desires but was synergistic and accommodating of all stakeholder needs. He didn't ignore the needs of the role, but he found creative ways to shape it, solving for his own desires by appropriating sufficient autonomy.

I learned a few rules from him:

1 Say yes to most opportunities. Roles are platforms for growth; they are not static lists of responsibilities.

2 Never decide on a role based on how it is currently being done or on who is doing the job.

3 Don't do the job you are given—do the job you were born to do.

Become a role shape shifter, and transform your roles to systematize your success.

Success Embodiment Trick #3: Talent Magnet

Achieving success, like raising a child, takes a village. Systematizing success requires systematic teaming. As your role increases in complexity, most challenges you face will require cross-functional solutions. That is why your teaming approach must not be limited by structure or current role assignments. Adopting a teaming approach that is both level blind and role blind. An approach that ignores reporting relationships and sees only synergies and opportunities. The network of people that support systematized success are abundant and varied.

I once did an exercise where I took a snapshot of my most prominent professional relationships. I made a list in Excel that included people I was working for, working with, or managing. I added some key suppliers, clients, and members of my network. Then I colour coded them green, yellow, or red.

- **Green** meant I would call them up for any reason.
- **Yellow** meant I would call them for a specific reason.
- **Red** meant I would hesitate to call them unless I had to.

I then looked at this list and tried to determine if there was a correlation to anything:

- Did the green list include people that I got along with? No.
- Did the red list include people that were mean? No.
- Was the list primarily hierarchical? No.

It was truthfully a confusing list until I thought about talent.

As I looked at the list of greens, it was filled with people whose talent I admired. With the yellows, I respected their talent but mostly in specific domains, and the reds I didn't appreciate or understand their talent but I needed to work with them.

I set out that month to work more with the greens and become more curious about the talents of the yellows and reds. What followed was a serious uplift in my satisfaction in my work over a period of approximately six months.

Simply by thinking of myself as a talent detective changed every interaction I had. And as a result, I was able to do the following:

- Identify and benefit from newly identified teachers
- Delegate better and develop my people in a much more inspiring way
- Build advocacy and sponsorship for my initiatives

Systematized success is not attainable without others, but it is not just about being surrounded by people that you can direct or that lead you to opportunities; it is also about being surrounded by people who bring out your talents and refresh their own. And it is always reciprocal. If you see and feel their talent, over time, they will be attracted to yours.

During a coaching session, sometimes my client will discover a new opportunity or goal they are enthusiastic about pursuing. To support them in planning the next step, I might ask them: "Who inspires you that you may want to explore this opportunity with?"

When they identify someone, I can't help but get excited and encourage them to commit to reaching out to them. Often enough they will hesitate, suggesting that they would need to confirm the other person's interest and priorities, check their mandates, etc. I will clarify: "I don't want you to ask them. I want you to attract them."

To ask would be a distraction from the desired approach because in order to ask the person, they would need to predefine an "ask", which requires positioning what they have in mind. This will already bias the collaboration. You are not asking for anything. You are simply attracting their talents to mutually exciting growth opportunities. Magnets attract magnetic material without elaborate discussion. Talent magnets do the same, strengthening each other through their collaborations.

Identify, nurture, and collaborate with other talent.

Success Embodiment Trick #4: Perpetual Renewal

One thing that I retained from my tenure at 3M was the culture of spending 15% of my worktime developing my own ideas. I remember being introduced to the 15% rule in my employee orientation with the facilitator saying, "If you're not working 15% of your time on something your boss doesn't know about, you're not doing your job." The 15% time program was launched by 3M in 1948 and is an embedded part of the culture. For the most part, it is fully optional and unmonitored, but it provides a permission slip to all employees to use a portion of their paid time to chase rainbows. 3M credits this program for producing many of the company's best-selling products. It is also cited for inspiring many similar programs at top technology companies decades later. Whether or not your employer embraces this philosophy shouldn't stop everyone from applying the concept. In fact, it didn't stop me from continuing to tap into the policy to bolster my engagement and impact long after I left 3M.

In my experience, the secrecy and deliberate absence of accountability in the 15% program is key to its power. This confidentiality helps to protect the early and critical elements of germinating an idea. Even the most brilliant creations are fragile at the start. They are vulnerable to criticism and resistance because we are vulnerable to feelings of rejection. In the early days of development, the quiet fortification of the idea is most important, and for that, you will want to find the most welcoming targeted environment in which to do so.

This can be akin to seeking the most fertile ground for your initiative. Farmers, for example, complete soil analysis and perform crop rotation to optimize the yield of their farms. Within your organization or your ecosystem of professional collaborators, you want to consider many options when deciding where you pursue the initiative. It is natural to resist pursuing options outside of your preferences, but be wary if you are considering only one implementation option. For your seed to grow into a stable enough seedling, nutrition and nurturing matter a lot.

Remember that your first environment is your most important one as the heartiness of your creation will depend on the health of your prototype.

Once you have a fairly robust aspiration, you will want to begin looking for alignment and synergies with other parallel initiatives or trends. The most successful leaders find ways to seamlessly align their initiative to the most current and active trends currently at play. This requires communication finesse, for the most part, by incorporating a compelling and relevant message that links your goal to a recognized important and urgent priority.

Now the challenge that you may face—even if the initiative is brilliantly aligned at the start—is that environments are not static. They are constantly reacting and shifting, making it necessary to follow their dance. All organizations or even customers, for example, experience "pendulum swings" or overcorrections to events or behaviours. Since there is no perfect business model, the leaders will deem it appropriate to deliberately shift the organization or group of people in a new direction every one to three years. The intent of the new direction is generally to harvest untapped opportunities or reduce unintended ramifications of the current model, but the difficulty for the individuals subjected to these pendulum swings is that it may make their initiatives more or less relevant. This is where savvy leaders find ways to creatively accommodate the pendulum swings by remaining relevant in the changing context.

This can involve reshaping or shifting priorities to strengthen the alignment to the strategic orientation of the key stakeholders. For some people, this may feel traumatic, as though they are compromising their ideals or watering down their impact. The savvy leader knows that shifting priorities is necessary and possible. They ask themselves, "How can I align with this WHILE improving my objective?" They keep working that question until they have answers, wasting no time on resisting the trend and knowing that the momentum from the wave of change has the potential to bolster their initiatives. They tap into their creativity, seek input, and search for insights and more advocates.

Incremental and ongoing success requires a willingness to release attachment to how we thought things were going to proceed and to be ever willing to revisit the facts. It requires wasting no time bemoaning uncontrollable events and spending more time seeking out new actionable opportunities.

Success Embodiment Trick #5: Broadcasting

The final step of the success embodiment tip is to go public. Boldly create visibility even if you don't need it, want it, or like it. I cannot count the number of times my clients have told me that they don't need visibility or credit, that they don't need the glory, and that they are in it for the "right" reasons. These same people beam and benefit when public recognition is cast on them. When, despite their opposition, they are publicly recognized, their experience serves as inspiration to others, they get exposed to future collaborators, they get access to more resources, and they stand taller. Every time.

I get the resistance—I remember feeling like I was busy enough doing my job, I didn't have the time or inclination to market myself. I resisted opportunities for recognition, brushing off praise or not absorbing it when others insisted. In a particularly dramatic moment, I barked at my boss, when he urged me to create more visibility for myself. I wanted a promotion and he was simply reminding me that the leadership team rarely promotes people they don't know. He said: "They need to see you in action, know about the great work you are doing." I protested insisting that self-promotion felt like prostitution, and I had no interest in doing it. Luckily for me, I had a few stubborn and generous sponsors that created exposure for me, despite my protests, to their credit , their advocacy contributed significantly to my ascension to leadership positions.

I now absolutely see the insanity in my actions because every time I have been generous enough to step into the light, amazing opportunities have opened up to me. I realize now that it is self-sabotage to hide, and that this world needs to see me being my best self. Assuming you recognize yourself in my behaviour, I would like to support you in reframing seeking out visibility. Your success requires you to become a broadcaster. If it doesn't, then you are not aiming high enough! To follow through with this, you need to reshape your WHY.

Why broadcast? I will give you five reasons:

1. To celebrate your co-contributors

Do it for altruistic reasons. It is far less enjoyable to be part of a team with a leader that shuns recognition. It limits the sense of appreciation that the entire team feels. You cannot belittle your accomplishments without belittling your teams. Celebrate your accomplishments and share the celebration with your team. Becoming a broadcaster of your team's results is one of the most generous acts a leader can do.

2. To inspire others

There is a reason people watch award shows and read autobiographies of great achievers—and it is not for entertainment purposes. We watch and read about them because it is inspiring to see other people achieving their dreams. It deepens our own aspirations and strengthens our commitment to ourselves. It fuels us during tough patches. Giving others an opportunity to see your success, inspires them. This world cannot afford for us to be stingy when it comes to supplying inspiration.

3. To integrate and accelerate your learning

A lesser known benefit to broadcasting is that it deepens your own development. Each time I support my clients in a recognition event, the mere act of preparation is of enormous value to them. The reflection on the lessons learned and the insights summarized to encapsulate the experience all support my client in integrating new competencies and increasing their confidence. We can miss our learning if we don't acknowledge it. When we acknowledge it, it becomes part of our belief system and our identity, providing us with a higher platform from which to launch our next initiative.

4. To re-create yourself

Another positive by-product of a broadcast is that it provides closure and publicly declares readiness for more. It consciously and subconsciously states, "Been there, done that, ready for more," and begs for new beginnings to take you higher. When my clients state that they feel stuck and that their pleasure in their work is dwindling, I immediately think it is a call to celebrate. I urge them to determine how they can celebrate in order to get unstuck. It can be as simple as celebrating a work anniversary, but in so doing, it creates a before and an after—an opportunity to profile their experience and skills, to open up new possibilities. Feeling stuck? Plan a launch party for a new you.

5. To initiate new relationships and new avenues

This last benefit from your broadcasting efforts will happen effortlessly. It is automatic and only requires your follow-up so that you can fully experience it. Celebrations by design, often include a broader set of individuals to interact with. With that broader set of individuals comes an extensive network of ideas and collaborators. It is rare that this interaction doesn't present an opportunity for a new relationship or path. Celebrations and appreciation events create the perfect neurochemistry that generates involuntary attraction to new opportunities.

So define your unique success definition, shift your identity, and apply these success embodiment tricks to make it happen.

COACHING EXERCISE

SUCCESS DEFINITION

Identify 8 areas that make up your success definition and score
your current state:

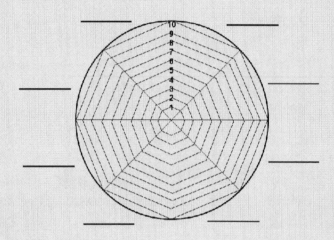

IDENTITY SHIFT

My identity shift: ....

From: ....

To: ....

Role Model: ....

RELEVANT EXPERIENCES

Past experiences to leverage: ....

....

Skills to apply: ....

....

People I will attract help from: ....

....

NOTES

W	WELL
O	OPPORTUNITY-ORIENTED
R	RELATIONSHIP-DRIVEN
K	KIND

S	SUCCESSFUL
M	MANAGERIAL
A	ACTION-ORIENTED
R	RESILIENT
T	TENACIOUS

MANAGERIAL

Management Matters

This critical part of the WORK SMART formula may not be trendy. The reality is that the term "manager" has gotten a bad rap over the last few years. Numerous expressions to contrast the difference between management and leadership has shifted our attention from management techniques to leadership attributes.

The reason for this shift is that management activities, although critical, are insufficient on their own, especially in managing knowledge workers.

In addition, some poor management styles were tolerated for years, my two least favourite being dictatorial (a manager who forces their way) and, on the other side of the spectrum, highly bureaucratic managers (a style that dramatically slows progress down). Thankfully these two styles are fading away. Market forces are bankrupting the bureaucrats, and highly skilled new talent is gravitating towards charismatic and consultative managers, thus abandoning the dictatorial style.

So although the term managerial may not feel like a compliment, it is not synonymous with an archaic, old model. It is still critical to your success.

There are a couple of reasons why I believe it is critical to the WORK SMART formula. The word "manage" has an impressive number of synonyms that I believe are important to any career, including guide, oversee, organize, conduct, and handle.

For most leaders, these activities are somewhat easier to master when applied to managing machinery or very simple tangible output. They can be less obvious today with the majority of our economy depending on knowledge workers. Knowledge workers being humans with humans' output and quality being more correlated with motivation and less so with how well the work was assigned or evaluated.

One hurdle for traditional managers is to overcome their underlying belief that motivation should be inherent in having a job and that the monetary compensation and security of employment is motivation enough. Given that we are living in the most abundant time in human history, for most employees today, this basic survival need simply does not register. Of course people need to pay their bills and provide for their families, but most people are confident that they can easily earn enough to provide for these basic needs in any job, so just having a job doesn't provide sufficient incentive.

In fact, most studies have proven that money is not a great motivator nor does it even increase our happiness above an estimated $50–$75K in annual income. [20] In fact, management matters more, and having a poor relationship with an immediate manager is consistently the top-cited reason for employees quitting their jobs. [21]

So what does it take to master management? Here are the top six focus areas that are most important:

1. **Model** – High productivity and efficiency
2. **Guide** – Beyond task to talent management
3. **Oversee** – Start fires and fuel them
4. **Organize** – Plan for dynamic environments
5. **Conduct**– Set the vision and foster meaning
6. **Handle** – Manage stress (yours and others')

Management Practice #1: Model – High Productivity and Efficiency

For the most part, slow-moving bureaucratic managers have been eliminated from the succession plans at most organizations. Market dynamics require managers today to be highly responsive to constant change. The context for a leader today includes an unprecedented pace of change, growing uncertainty, and pressure to react quickly to market feedback. Stagnation or resistance to change is not an option, making it imperative for managers to create highly productive and efficient cultures.

Most managers are already highly productive people. They master how to manage their time and tasks and build processes for sustained output. They hone this skill set such that they are able to produce impressive output that enables them to ascend to a management position. As their responsibilities continue to scale up, however, many managers see a breaking point, where they can no longer scale in the same way. New strategies must emerge in order for them to master managing highly productive and efficient teams that can produce most of the output.

As these managers switch from being productive themselves to creating a team of productive people, it becomes important to develop a new kind of PLAN.

P **Priority:** Unceasing focus on identifying the highest-value activities; clarifying and assigning resources and progressing on these priorities

L **Leverage:** Constructing an ecosystem of talent pools to leverage while developing effective delegation and governance skills

A **Accountability:** Unwavering commitment to self and others that generates predictable and reliable delivery and quality

N **Now:** Time allocation mentality and discipline that favours completing activities early, valuing progress today over tomorrow

I find the best way to support my clients to shift their habits around this P.L.A.N. is to support them in creating a ritual around their daily activities and tasks. I worked with Nick Greschner, Accenture Canada's HR Country Lead, to do just that. Nick was working on elevating himself and his team to best support the needs of a growing consulting practice. To create a new way of working we started with a top down approach where he identified the 4 key roles, that only he could do:

1) Chief Talent Manager
2) Chief Culture & Engagement Lead
3) Talent Brand Ambassador
4) Chief People Developer

From there he mapped out the mission statement for each role to clarify his ambition (**P**riority), then he named the individuals he would leverage to achieve that mission (**L**everage), followed by the specific outcome defined by measurable results (**A**ccountability) and then scheduled time each week with targeted tasks each day that would ensure that he was making progress in each key area (**N**ow). When leaders create clarity and model these precise behaviours, their teams achieve steady productivity that is undeterred by the turbulence of change.

Management Practice #2: Guide – Beyond Task to Talent Management

The traditional view of a manager's value is measured by outcomes, specifically, task completion. Is the task getting done, and is the outcome what we need? This emphasis on the outcome can orient management attention to the process or system yield, perhaps at the expense of paying attention to the people doing the work.

Managers who are unable to make a shift from managing tasks to managing people tend to limit their career progression since they fall prey to the tendency to control people in order to get the required output instead of developing and organizing their people to create the output. The problem with this approach, aside from demotivating the team, is that they cannot scale this way. Their career progression becomes limited by their time.

The talent manager's daily focus is different. They are constantly asking themselves, "Are the individuals set up for success?" A focus on talent management shifts their orientation from the task to the worker, seeing that every task is an opportunity to develop and enhance the skills in their team. This has them assigning work designed not only to get the job done but to elevate the individual while the work is being done. This manager focuses on creating growth opportunities while setting their people up for success.

Focusing on the health of the talent, in addition to the health of the process, bolsters the quality of the output. It also engenders a sustainable culture, where people look out for each other and collaborate well. When the leader models consideration for how individuals are holding up, team members begin to pay attention to how they are impacting each other.

Managing talent requires a keen eye on how individuals are performing in their roles and how the team is performing in overlapping responsibilities. A talent manager notices what individuals and teams need in order to progress efficiently. They resolve role ambiguity that challenges accountability. They attune themselves to prompting deadlines, chunking down large deliverables into achievable milestones and holding quality reviews well in advance of final deadlines.

It also requires creating work norms that serve the best interest of the entire team. Building agreements between all team members, asking them to identify and commit to behaviours that set-up collaborations for the best outcome. Whether this includes rules about multitasking, smart phone usage or how people listen to each other in meetings; the more the leader supports creating the best environment for the team, the better the team will perform.

When you manage the talent that manages the deliverables, your focus is on creating the environment for the team to succeed rather than imposing an approach or doing the work for them.

Management Practice #3: Oversee – Start Fires and Fuel Them

Managers set the direction and priorities for the team. They then have to quickly shift to overseeing the efforts of the team by liaising with other groups, instilling the appropriate sense of urgency and removing any impediments to progress.

This at times, includes moving aside themselves and getting out of the team's way while maintaining appropriate oversight.

Managers who ignite their teams spark fires that get people's attention, making them feel highly relevant and worthwhile. They unite and focus their team on priorities that are relatable and recognizable so that their people remain in action.

To ensure sustained action, however, smart managers recognize the need to fuel the fire. Rather than having to be the one to continuously feed the fire, a savvy manager recognizes that the most important part of their oversight responsibility is to support the team with enough energy to fuel their success.

Liz Ryan, CEO and founder of Human Workplace, summarizes this growing need in an article in Forbes, where she states, "For years we pretended that human energy isn't a factor in a team's success, even though anybody who has ever been on any kind of team knows that the team energy is the whole ballgame!" [22]

Sustained Energy for the Team = Their Fuel

Fuel comes in many forms, but I find leaders benefit from paying closer attention to the following four areas in particular:

- Enjoying the process
- Celebrating the progress
- Giving and receiving recognition
- Discovering new opportunities

Creating a highly energized team:

	DO	DON'T
Enjoying the process	Aim to make the work environment pleasant and enjoyable. Demonstrate interest in accommodating needs.	Don't ignore easy-to-resolve pain points or irritants simply because they may be temporary.
Celebrating the progress	Keep track of past milestones and completion-to-date; acknowledge and make visible the significant progress that has been made.	Don't immediately shift to new priorities, ignoring preceding milestones. Don't reinforce how much is yet to come rather than seeing how far the team has come.
Giving and receiving recognition	Encourage both formal and informal recognition. Include scheduled recognition events, and be open to making time for celebrating in any and all team interactions.	Don't limit recognition to subordinates (include leaders, peers, and direct reports), but encourage people to recognize each other regardless of hierarchy. Don't cancel or skip scheduled recognition events.
Discovering new opportunities	Support your people in noticing the unfolding of new opportunities through their efforts. Celebrate discoveries, growth, and possibilities that link to their efforts.	Don't avoid or limit the scope of initiatives such that it isolates the team. Remain open to synergies that may lead to future benefits.

Management Practice #4: Organize – Plan for Dynamic Environments

Management is absolutely about achieving specific objectives and meeting requirements—the static results. But even the most stable markets and products can no longer rely on a static view. This static world with a goal of achieving process perfection to be repeated over and over again no longer represents reality.

Establishing robust processes, systems, and structures remains an important management execution priority, but today's environment is far from static as rapid change touches every aspect of the value chain. The ability to innovate and evolve in a dynamic world is now an imperative.

To be effective at managing these dynamics, a leader needs to have one foot in today and one foot in tomorrow. This means having clear priorities and focusing on today's objectives while being informed, responsive, and bold in planning for tomorrow's. This requires creating space for tomorrow despite the presence of an overwhelming number of details to react to that are sufficient to consume the entire day.

A manager who does not reserve time for high value, non-urgent activities is doomed to fail. To do this consistently, you need to structure it into your daily priorities and routines.

For many people, this is a real challenge since reactive activities consume them; it is worse for their teams since working for a reactive leader can be toxic. So how can you consistently, day after day, reserve sufficient time for the future? By making it a habit.

Most leaders agree that the best time to work on future-oriented activities is in the morning, when your mind and body are rested and your thinking is clearer. They also benefit from keeping long-term goals visible by writing them down and reviewing them daily. They let themselves get excited about the future, no matter how busy or reactive their day gets, and this grounds them and helps them avoid becoming overwhelmed.

Today's dynamic and complex environment requires more than static planning. It requires leaders who take the time to proactively envision the future and position their teams with options that will support the attainment of their success.

Management Practice #5: Conduct – Set the Vision and Foster Meaning

For over 15 years, I played violin in an orchestra which is probably why I love using the analogy of a conductor to reflect on management today. In contrast to a drill sergeant shouting out directions, an orchestra conductor waves a baton and cues the entries, exits, and dynamics of the specialty skills on the team.

The manager's equivalent "orchestra baton" is a shared vision which serves to provide direction to their knowledge workers.

Establishing and communicating a big, audacious goal for your department or team is one of the most important aspects of the job. It unites your team around a goal that they can take pride in achieving together. The more spectacular the vision, the more your team will feel proud to be a part of it and welcome the opportunity. During the unveiling of the vision, the excitement and energy should be felt by everyone.

The smart manager understands that the power of the vision relies on its meaningfulness to every member of the team. What does the vision mean for them? What is their piece of it? How close do they feel to it? It is the meaningfulness of the vision that holds the team together on the prolonged journey.

Experienced workers know that journeys can be long, challenging, and fraught with detours, at times making even the destination itself subject to doubt. This is why smart leaders understand the importance of fostering and inspiring meaning throughout the journey to navigate these trials.

Fostering meaning that has staying power requires an approach that is both 1) deeply individualized and 2) embedded in the collective team spirit.

I feel like I know something about teaming. My employment in a management consulting company virtually guaranteed that even within a few short years, I would quickly lose track of the number of teams with which I worked. Delivering on outcomes with blended teams, including clients, vendors, and colleagues, with limited shared history, incentives, cultures, and geographies has taught me a few tricks.

The biggest mistake I have seen is that leaders skip over even the basics of team building in a rush to achieve outcomes often minimizing the importance of meaning and team spirit.

What I will share here is a recipe to consistently create a well-functioning team with members that energize one another.

First, here's the recipe for team spirit:

Individual's Sense of Feeling Valued + Appreciation for Fellow Team Members = Team Spirit

The exercise below is easy to do and helps to create both individual meaning and team spirit. Here are the steps:

1   Ask each team member to prepare responses to these three questions:

> a) What is a professional accomplishment that you are very proud of? Come prepared to share why.
> b) Can you share some of the ways you made it happen?
> c) What are some of the similarities with our new mandate?

2 Call a meeting, and ask people to take turns sharing one by one while everyone else makes a note of the positive attributes they hear in their colleague's story.

3 After the person has shared their responses, ask each of the other members to identify the attributes they observed and what was meaningful about the achievement and relevant current goals.

4 Wrap up the session by summarizing some of the common themes, but trust that the real work is already done.

This exercise generates a very real sense of feeling valued and stimulates appreciation for each other. The team will naturally be cognisant of others' ambitions. This simple exchange primes the team to collaborate on a new level, one that authentically encourages and supports everyone. A team's cohesion is like a spider web, its strength comes from the connections between the individuals. The best teams encourage each other to strengthen their ties on their own, through ongoing transparent dialogue and shared successes.

There are times, however, when most of the team is onboard but for one or two people. They may have sat quietly in the meeting but are later immersed in hallway dissension. This dynamic occurs when there is either an insufficient amount of goodwill or psychological safety for the team to sustain open dialogue.

Today's complex cross-functional team environments can make this more common, with diverse views requiring more dialogue to enable full alignment.

One tool that I learned during my coaching certification in Conversational Intelligence®[17] can be helpful in this context. The framework includes 5 common mindsets that individuals experience during a challenging discussion. These are:

- **Resistor** (Not open to influence)
- **Skeptic** (Consumed with doubt and vocal about it)
- **Wait and See** (On the fence, unable to take action)
- **Experi-Mentor** (Open to experiment, prototype or pilot)
- **Co-Creator** (Eager to move forward and contribute)

In a team coaching session, I teach my clients these mindsets prior to discussing a potentially contentious issue. When I introduce the mindsets, we all agree that these mindsets are normal and we promise that no one is to be made to feel wrong when their mindsets fluctuate during the discussion. While we all aspire to elevate ourselves towards the co-creating mindset, we commit to be self-aware and transparent in what mindset we are actually experiencing in the moment. We make it okay to articulate our needs and also accept responsibility to support each other in the process. Once the discussion is launched, it always amazes me how quickly the group engages and applies this new shared language to contextualize their opinions during the discussion. They will say things like: "I need everyone's help because my head is stuck in Resistor and let me share why..."

This transparency and shared language supports the leader to better direct and align the diverse opinions. Just like our conductor, allowing all the cross-functional skilled team members to express themselves, while supporting them in coming together to perform the symphony.

Management Practice #6: Handle – Manage Stress

There is nothing worse than working for a manager who cannot manage their own stress. Team members look to their leader to help them handle difficult situations. If the leader is freaking out, it is one of the most destabilizing factors there is.

Managing stress is also becoming more difficult. Today's context is more demanding. Leaders can no longer act calm while waiting for the storm to pass. Today's leaders need to be highly effective in an almost constant storm.

They are expected to master three elements simultaneously:

1. Have flawless execution of current priorities
2. Be highly responsive to market feedback
3. Drive innovation for the future

In other words, perform at your best despite a lot of uncertainty.

Uncertainty, as you know, is really hard on our brains. Our brains don't handle it that well. When we feel uncertain, our brains vacillate and bother us with worry, repetition, and iterations. They spin a lot.

The research on stress has been fascinating to follow. At first, it was very confusing to scientists because the commonly held belief was that all stress had a primarily negative effect on the body. The data suggested otherwise: Even if the physiological response in two individuals was very similar, there was a significant difference in whether the individuals reported feeling stressed.

Ultimately, it was determined that there is both positive and negative stress. The detrimental health impacts correlate with negative stress but not with positive stress.

What they concluded is that stress is either negative (damaging to our cells) or not based on our perception of the stress. Don't miss that—this is very useful. Your perception controls your experience of stress, so you can control your stress simply by controlling your perception.

Basically, here's how it works: If you perceive a threat and decide that the threat is bigger than your ability to meet the threat, then your body and behaviours will be subject to negative stress. Alternatively, if you decide that your resources are bigger than the threat, you will enter positive stress (called the challenge response), and the impact on your body and behaviours will not be negatively impacted.

You can literally transform your experience of stress by perceiving your abilities and resources as larger than the threat.

The study that I found most incredible in this area was one by the American Heart Association. In a study of 151 coronary heart disease patients, half of them were given stress rehabilitation in addition to physical rehabilitation following bypass surgery. The stress rehabilitation was simply a discussion with a therapist once per week, where the therapist reinforced positive messages about the treatment efficacy and the patient's recovery progress. At the end of the study, the rate of cardiac events such as heart attack, stroke, chest pains requiring hospitalization, or death was 33% for the participants who received only physical rehabilitation versus 18% for those who received stress rehabilitation. [23] The simple act of reminding patients of their resources once a week cut the risk by almost half during the follow-up period of three years. That is the impact of a more positive perception of a challenge.

Managing your stress as a manager and building stress management skills within your teams is incredibly important, and you can improve it significantly. When facing a challenge that could be stressful, simply take a moment to remember the resources that you can tap into to meet the threat.

Tip the balance on the scale towards your resources, and you will enable yourself to manage the situation with much more ease.

THREATS

RESOURCES

Skills
Past experience
Team members
Assets
Sponsors/Advocates

Remember that management matters, a lot, in fact. Apply these practices and you will be effective at elevating and scaling the output of your entire organization.

COACHING EXERCISE

TALENT FOCUSED
What do you want to do more, or less of?

Do More

- ○ Improve work environment
- ○ Accommodate needs
- ○ Celebrate progress
- ○ Give recognition
- ○ Seek opportunities
- ○ ....

Do Less

- ○ Ignore pain points
- ○ Forget progress made
- ○ Miss recognition events
- ○ Limit initiative
- ○ Isolate the team
- ○ ....

VISION
Define your biggest, most audacious vision for your team:

....

....

....

TEAMING
Plan your next team-building event:

....

....

....

STRESS MANAGEMENT:
Reflect on an area of responsibility where you are prone to stress.
Identify resources available to you to meet the challenge:

....

....

....

NOTES

W WELL

O OPPORTUNITY-ORIENTED

R RELATIONSHIP-DRIVEN

K KIND

S SUCCESSFUL

M MANAGERIAL

A ACTION-ORIENTED

R RESILIENT

T TENACIOUS

ACTION-ORIENTED

Subjects in Motion Stay in Motion

We've all experienced it—the feeling of getting stuck. One minute we're discussing, planning, and doing things...and then something happens. There is inertia, gravity, resistance, and lethargy. We feel unable to take action.

Sometimes the feeling is triggered by an external event, such as hearing news or experiencing an event that puts into question our path.

Sometimes this is a result of seeing disappointing results, like reviewing metrics and acknowledging that we have fallen short of meeting our expectations. We can't deny them; they are staring us in the face.

Sometimes it is triggered by hearing or seeing someone else's results: We see someone else's perceived success and compare it to our own progress, and it just wipes us out. Even if we deeply respect and admire the person, we compare and feel envious and frustrated with ourselves.

The problem, of course, is that our success requires ongoing action, so despite these frequent and natural occurrences, the ability to dust ourselves off and get back into action is absolutely critical.

When we are working smart, we naturally get into action as we enthusiastically focus on achieving our dreams. And yet, there are the days when the obstacles appear bigger and stronger than our resolve. To maintain our action orientation in the face of these obstacles takes some practice and tools. Being quipped to deal with setbacks, discouraging events and general malaise is critical to your success. Without these tools you will be forced to rely too much on your willpower. Willpower is finite and gets consumed very quickly. These action orientations are renewable and will organically support you to get you through tough times. Getting you back on your horse quickly, whenever you fall off.

Here we will cover six critical action orientations:

1. Have a powerful relationship with facts
2. Avoid overthinking
3. Stop worrying so much
4. Compare only for inspiration
5. Watch your reasoning
6. Build your activation team

Action Orientation #1: Have a Powerful Relationship with Facts

Facts are important. They provide the tangible evidence of our effort. This tangible evidence represents the accumulated accomplishments of our past—the fully baked, completed accomplishments, not the ones in the oven. They represent our past but also hint at our future—at least the future extrapolated from the platform we have established.

For these reasons, I'm not a fan of ignoring the facts. I am a big fan of documenting our goals and milestones and evaluating our results against these as an important and systematic check-in.

This includes having a powerful relationship with financials, business cases, and metrics, your personal ones and the professional ones for which you are the steward.

The facts, however, can be confusing or upsetting—confusing if you abdicate your responsibility to own them, understand them, and make sense of them and upsetting at times since they may underrepresent the opportunities in the future. The facts only represent the past, the fully baked goods, even if you have a boatload of goodies in the oven and a truckload of ingredients in the mix master. Your work-in-progress is important and a leading indicator but since there is no guarantee that the goodies will make it to a paying customer, they don't show up in the facts.

Having a powerful (and not paralyzing) relationship with facts and figures means that you understand their importance and you honour what they are indicating while recognizing that they do not fully represent the whole picture.

Generally, I find that my clients, when in a healthy mindset, are able to maintain a very pragmatic and healthy relationship with facts as long as they can separate them from elaborate interpretations. All of us have a tendency at times to entangle our review of the facts with elaborate interpretations, and it is these interpretations that can halt our actions.

For example, you receive your revenue figures for your division, product, or business, and they are lower than expected. You are extremely disappointed because you believed that this month was going to be better. You're extremely frustrated, and you start questioning yourself, your team, your competence, others' integrity...you name it. These are the interpretations that you are weaving around the numbers. At this point, you are increasingly upset and completely immobilized and entangled by your thoughts and worries. These interpretations lead you further away from being in a position to take any reasonable action.

To remedy a circumstance like this, I instruct my clients to play a game called "Act, Fact, and Interpret" in order to get over the situation quickly and get back into action.

The exercise is simple but amazing. It helps you to quickly evaluate the situation more objectively by separating facts from interpretations and planning your next action based on facts only. This will help you reduce anxieties that drain you of energy so that you can face the situation.

In this exercise, facts are facts (meaning they have happened and can be independently verified). Interpretations include anything that has not yet happened, any assumptions in your head, and often times many exaggerations that you could not possibly have validated.

The act section you leave blank (for now) as you detail out the facts and separate them from all interpretations. Then, ignoring the interpretations and looking only at the facts, plan your next action steps.

Notice, in the example below, how the interpretations are more likely to cause you to behave indecisively, and paralyze you - much more so than dealing with the facts. It is actually quite easy to identify the appropriate next steps when the facts are isolated from your interpretations.

ACT	FACT	INTERPRETATION
Analyze the numbers.	Revenue is lower than expected.	You're failing.
		This project is never going to work.
Rally the team. Meet with top clients.		
		You're in trouble. Someone dropped the ball.
		Your team is not committed.

Now, that you have a place to store your interpretations, you can focus entirely on taking the first action step. Once you are in action, the interpretations will further melt away and will be replaced by information from the real world. This exercise helps you get there faster because the intermingling of facts with interpretations is what causes you to slow down.

Action Orientation #2: Avoid Overthinking

"How long have you been thinking about this?" I will ask innocently. I will hear, "It's been spinning around my head for weeks." Spin, the most frustrating of all thinking states, is repetitive, ongoing and seemingly unending, and often even sleep depriving.

In an attempt to find the perfect answer, our minds ruminate and ruminate. The thing is, there likely isn't a perfect answer, which is what makes the whole process futile. All the overthinking is perhaps just an exercise in trying to manipulate information to try to make us feel better about an imperfect but necessary decision.

It makes us feel better when the outer world corresponds to what we want or think it should be—but it rarely does.

So the first trick is to release our perfectionistic tendencies to seek a perfect answer. The easiest way to do this is to tap into acceptance—accepting the situation and circumstances for what they are and surrendering to the possibility that imperfections are noble and necessary. There is wisdom that will surface that can only be revealed through the imperfection—not wisdom that you are assured of understanding but wisdom that may someday reveal itself to you.

After accepting and embracing the imperfection, you're likely ready to look at the situation objectively. Do you have all the information you require, or do you need further external perspectives—not internal (that's your thinking) but external, like input from others, research, or data analysis? Follow your curiosity until you feel satisfied and complete in your reflection.

Then, still without thinking, I recommend sitting with the situation for five long, quiet minutes and feeling the call to action grow—the call to action within you that knows it is time to act and knows exactly what to do.

Trust me, your call to action is in there, and once it surfaces, you will feel that alignment you needed and feel brave enough to move—then just do it!

Action Orientation #3: Stop Worrying So Much

I admit that I am guilty of worrying too much. In fact, before all my keynote speeches, I plan to arrive a couple of hours before simply to worry for at least an hour before going onstage. In that case, it's more strategic worrying since I like to arrive early to avoid the stress of arriving late, but not all of my worries are strategic, more often than not.... Worry is my sneaky way to procrastinate.

If you, too, are a worrier, you probably have trouble stopping it. It's not like we choose to worry. Worrying is a natural instinct— our minds are constantly scanning for threats, right? Yes, but worry can become unhealthy when we allow our minds to dwell on perceived threats without taking action.

This happens to me when I get tricked into believing that my worrying is productive thinking. As though the worrying is helping me think through a problem. I only realize the flaw in this theory when my absence of progress smells of something else I know all too well—procrastination.

Just like organizing your desk to avoid working on that proposal, worrying is an active distraction from acting on your priorities. It's important for you to quickly catch yourself in this spin and get back in the game. The best way to stop worrying is to simply take action.

Here are some examples of common worrying traps to help you catch yourself:

Worrying instead of asking:
This worry trap happens when you find yourself able to articulate concerns (including elaborate details of risks and implications) for initiatives that are outside of your direct control. The degree of detail in the thinking demonstrates that you have given it way too much thought without having a direct conversation with the individuals

actually driving the work. This worry evaporates as soon as you reach out to the stakeholders and ask questions to determine the current state and decide whether you can contribute or not.

Worrying instead of progressing:

This worry trap often occurs when we start to allow our thinking to expand outside the discernable timeframe, thus distracting us from taking the most appropriate next step (extreme example: worrying about the university your child is going attend while they are still in diapers). This worry can be stopped in its tracks by simply focusing on the very next step and taking action.

Worrying instead of helping:

Some of the most difficult worries to deal with are worries that make us feel helpless, like an illness or tragedy that we are witnessing that devastates us. We worry for those most impacted, and we feel helpless and don't know what to do. But once again, our suffering is prolonged by our inactivity. Any small act of kindness, showing compassion, donating to the cause, or mobilizing a response will do wonders for our spirits.

Worrying is an energy waster, you don't want to waste the precious energy that fuels your actions. Now you can avoid the most common worrying traps so they won't fool you next time.

Action Orientation #4: Compare for Inspiration

Many people are unconsciously thrown into mood-altering comparison without a moment's notice. Comparison is also an action killer.

A very brief scroll through any social media site can literally throw otherwise amazingly talented people off of their game for hours. Comparison sneaks up on us. It takes our eyes off of our game and distracts us. There's a reason why race horses wear blinders to block their peripheral vision; it is so that they focus on running their own best race.

Still, comparison is natural and impossible to fully avoid, so most people require a strategy. The first strategy is to know when you are in it. This is less obvious than one may think because I've come to notice that comparison sneaks up on us through our judgements of ourselves or others. When we catch ourselves making a judgement about an activity or achievement that someone else is doing or seeking, and we hear ourselves either wanting it (envy) or disapproving of it (disgust), we are in the act of comparing.

And once we start comparing, we need to make a choice: Are we going to be inspired by their journey or stand in judgement of it?

If we stand in judgement of them, convinced that either they don't deserve it or shouldn't want what they are seeking, then we shrink what is possible for us. In a strange attempt to limit them, we end up limiting ourselves.

The alternative is to be inspired by it. "Inspired by it?" some of my clients will inquire. "Even if I don't agree with it?" Yes. You don't need to agree with their dreams or stand in judgement of what they desire. You need only celebrate since their achievement is demonstrative of what your achievement will be. It won't look the same—it will be unique to you, just as theirs is unique to them—but it will be equally glorious.

When we allow ourselves to be inspired by others, we say to ourselves, "If they can do that, what could I do?" allowing our own striving to grow. We also might see opportunities for collaborations that our judgements would have completely masked. Simply by asking, "If they can do that, what could we do together?"

Transforming the experience of comparison and learning to celebrate and fuel your own objectives creates much more ease for the smart worker.

It's easier than you think; just follow these steps:

1 Notice when you are vulnerable to comparison.

2 Tap into your appreciation of what they have achieved, resisting any judgement.

3 Choose to be inspired by it.

4 Determine how their success may bolster yours, either directly or indirectly.

5 Notice how much more fun it is to be inspired by others, and reward yourself.

Action Orientation #5: Watch Your Reasoning

I know this may sound obnoxious but your reasoning is biased and flawed. It's true. Everyone's reasoning is completely polluted by our cognitive bias. We're not alone—even rats, birds, and monkeys have cognitive bias. The evolutionary purpose of this bias is to help us survive.

For example, our negativity bias causes us to give more weight to negative experiences than to positive ones. That's because in unsafe environments, avoiding danger made our ancestors more likely to survive. We are also biased to maintain a relatively good opinion of ourselves; this makes us willing to ignore evidence when we make mistakes, presumably so that we can forgive ourselves. Finally, we are biased for efficiency to reduce the effort of analyzing information. In fact, if you let it, your brain will take shortcuts—called heuristics—that will lead you to irrational conclusions.

Since we cannot reliably count on our reasoning in and of itself, it is important for us to demand evidence from ourselves to support our decision-making process.

The process of requesting and evaluating evidence from ourselves and others is part of working smart.

Just think about this very simple sentence structure (expressed often in our thoughts as well as in our words): "I was going to... but..." followed by very sophisticated and interesting reasons.

These reasons often include explanations that support your conclusion. Now ask yourself, "What evidence do I have for that?" You will be surprised how many times you simply say,

"Well, that's what I think."

Reasoning without evidence from the outside world is subject to cognitive bias. The most revealing clue that your reasoning is polluted by cognitive bias is when your reasons justify inaction.

For example:

- The client is not responsive; they're obviously not interested in our proposal.
- I reviewed the job opportunity, and I don't have the experience they need.
- I was going to share my perspective, but the meeting was running late.

Statements that justify inaction are often fabricated, to avoid effort.

To unleash your potential and stay in action, it is important to be highly suspect of any reason that justifies inaction. Call yourself out, and get some evidence before you blindly follow your bias.

Action Orientation #6: Build Your Activation Team

Here's the important thing about action orientation and your support system: There are people who spring us into action and people who help us rest and relax. It's important to know the difference, and part of your robust action orientation is to call on the right one in the right situation. Most of us have people in our lives that perform a version of these roles:

1. **Energizer:** Get you moving even when you don't want to
2. **Zen buddy:** Help you rest and recover
3. **Comic relief:** Make you laugh until you just don't care
4. **Worry warrior:** Support you in avoiding risk and navigating it when you can't avoid it
5. **Cheerleader:** People that see you as amazing, capable, and invincible

All of these roles can be important in our quest to remain action oriented. We benefit from interaction with others to sustain our momentum. We also need the foresight and discipline to reach out to the right person.

For years, this messed me up. When I felt sad and lethargic, I would call my Zen buddy. She would reassure me and confess that she didn't get why I was so driven in the first place. I would hang up the phone confused. On the other hand, she was amazing when I called her after finishing a big project. Then she had just what I needed, a little rest and recovery and I was fully re-energized.

My comic relief friends are particularly helpful at taking the pressure off, when I need it. They provide temporary relief making me laugh until I am able to decompress just enough to reduce my stress and reignite my passion for my goals.

The Energizer bunnies get me moving and shed any lethargic behaviour. And in times of crisis, I am lost without my worry warriors. They know all the risks to manage. They have a plan in mind, one that they have been conceiving for years to quickly get me out of trouble and protect me from harm.

To get me fully unstuck professionally, it is the cheerleader that I often need the most. These individuals include colleagues, clients, bosses, sponsors, and advocates—people who have seen me doing my best work and the ones that know with absolute certainty that no matter how desperate the situation may seem, I'm a mere moment away from returning to that greatness.

Sustained action requires sustained networks that are capable of charging you up when you feel a little low.

Your activation team can also help you with a particularly plaguing experience known as shame. Shame occurs following a regretful experience. Moments in time when you were not able to be your best professional self. Meetings that you could have led better. Conversations that you could have handled better. Emotionally charged situations that you could have navigated better or mistakes that you have made.

Depending on your sensitivity, some of these experiences may have been easy to address directly. Some you might have chosen to shake off. Others may have wiped out your productivity for a few hours.

The worst experiences are the ones that we think make us look bad, these make us what to hide and isolate ourselves.

We also tend to repress our emotions in these moments but that too will come back to bite us in sneaky ways. In the form of avoiding situations or people, in irrational decisions, in unsubstantiated biases— basically, ways that can seem subtle but over time erode our leadership and our action orientation.

This is why I was so drawn to Brené Brown's work. In her book, The Gifts of Imperfection, I related to the need to banish shame since it is particularly lethal for action orientation. Her work concludes that shame festers on secrecy. If we are embarrassed and we hide our regrets or mistakes, they grow. Shame cannot tolerate transparency and empathy.[24] Particularly with people who admire and love you, like the members of your activation team. The minute we expose our vulnerability and mistakes to others and receive the reassurance that (although we may have made a mistake) this does not make us a bad person, shame evaporates.

Your unprecedented success depends on maintaining your action orientation. This is what will make you unstoppable. It only requires applying these strategies to keep up your momentum and avoid applying the brakes.

COACHING EXERCISE

REASONING

Choose a situation that you are struggling to resolve. Use the template below to document all of the facts and the associated interpretations. Once you have completed untangling the facts from the interpretations, plan your act steps (based only on the facts).

ACT	FACT	INTERPRET

COMPARISON

Think about someone who annoys you in some way, either because of their accomplishments or because of the choices they are making in their life.

Identify what you find inspiring about them...and how they may bolster your motivation.

I am inspired by: ....

It bolsters my commitment to: ....

ACTIVATION TEAM

Identify the best people to call when you feel stuck and unable to take action in the following ways:

When I feel sad, I will call ....

When I feel lazy, I will call ....

When I am worried, I will call ....

When I feel ashamed, I will call ....

NOTES

W	**WELL**
O	**OPPORTUNITY-ORIENTED**
R	**RELATIONSHIP-DRIVEN**
K	**KIND**
S	**SUCCESSFUL**
M	**MANAGERIAL**
A	**ACTION-ORIENTED**
R	**RESILIENT**
T	**TENACIOUS**

RESILIENT

Preventing Burnout and Transforming Complacency

Most professionals whom I work with have very challenging roles. They have achieved their positions due in part to their ability to manage change and perform well under pressure. Sometimes I will ask them, "Are you having an invigorating or depleting day today?" Or "Is this week building your resiliency or depleting it?"

It is normal and to be expected in any challenging and rewarding career to have many days that feel depleting. Sometimes there is even a prolonged string of them. What's most important is that you take notice and keep track.

If your days are just your days, you mostly relate to feeling *fine* or *mildly frustrated*, and you have concluded that this is just part of the deal, then you may already be on your way down a slippery slope to either complacency or burnout.

Neither place you want to go to. Complacency is defined as accepting low standards even though there are clear deficiencies. Burnout, on the other hand, is harder to ignore, since it is characterised by a physical or mental collapse caused by overwork or stress.

Both result in a wholly involuntary loss of agency as though you have been flipped to autopilot and are reacting clumsily to external demands. Day after day of your professional life...half-heartedly doing your thing.

Most people know when they have a severely bad day marked by a specific event that culminates in anger, exhaustion, or sadness. They also have their preferred coping mechanisms, which could include alcohol, exercise, a bubble bath, or comfort food to numb the experience. The challenge is knowing when the acute experiences become chronic. Survival techniques become habits, and daily suffering becomes routine, leading to a solidified pattern that makes you work unconsciously.

Not only is it a waste of your precious talents but these periods erode your resiliency, making it impossible to strive for a new reality.

If you catch yourself living in the repetitive pattern of numbing your pain to survive your work, then you are living on borrowed time. Eventually a wave of challenges will come your way and knock you off your board; you will end up in a crisis, with little or no reserves built up to stabilize yourself.

This is when burnout typically gets diagnosed. A 2017 survey by Kronos Incorporated found that burnout is the number one cause of employee turnover. It is also expected to rise, with as much as 60% of employees citing high levels of stress, extreme fatigue, and a feeling of being out of control—all early signs of burnout. [25]

Burnout is preventable by proactively building resiliency. Smart workers protect themselves from burnout, and smart leaders take action to protect their teams.

This chapter covers five specific ways to increase your resilience so that you can engage in your work at the highest level:

1. Build your reserves to avert burnout
2. Reduce your reactivity
3. Create a prototype of a better you
4. Keep your saboteurs in check
5. Intervene early, and invest in your recovery

Resiliency Tip #1: Build Your Reserves

When I was a little girl, shortly after breakfast at our summer cottage (years before the availability of an online weather forecast), my sisters and I would stand around a weather barometer and fight over who got to tap it. It measured the barometric pressure and suggested with its movement whether we were headed to rain or to sunshine. It was not precise, but it was indicative.

When I think about monitoring resiliency, it reminds me of the nudging movement of the arrow. As humans, we are highly adaptive and can normalize almost any circumstance, which makes it difficult to be fully aware of whether we are sufficiently resilient or not. We can, however, notice whether our current experiences, environments, and choices are moving us in the right direction or the wrong direction.

Burnout does not happen overnight. The journey to burnout is long and preventable. It is caused by slippages in our footing. When it arrives in its debilitating form, the most common collection of symptoms includes feeling overwhelmed, insignificant, disconnected, and exhausted. Each of these can be averted by taking proactive steps.

Build Resiliency to Prevent Overwhelm

There are two main contributors that lead to overwhelm: 1) lack of focus or prioritization and 2) insufficient perceived progress against a growing workload.

In order to increase your resilience to being overwhelmed, two very simple concepts need to be mastered. The first relates to making choices. Your brain wants certainty. If it doesn't know what is most important right now, it gets very nonsensical.

For many professionals, prioritization and focus are extremely challenging with multiple reporting relationships and competing organizational priorities. Yet maintaining your resiliency depends on you deciding to empower yourself to make a choice for every moment, including 1) what you will focus on, 2) for how long, and 3) how you will manage interruptions. Then just doing it. Even if you feel uncertain whether you picked the right thing to focus on, the benefits to your state of mind will outweigh any future adjustments required. Just focus on completing the very next action.

The second necessary defense against becoming overwhelmed involves deliberately showing your mind that you are making progress. This can be progress against a milestone or even a long list of to-dos that are all crossed off. You need to see progress to combat feeling overwhelmed. For some knowledge workers, due to the nature of the thinking time that may go into a deliverable, progress may not feel tangible or linear. This exacerbates the sensation that we are not making sufficient progress. In these cases, you will want to create mini-milestones that provide your mind with visibility to progress, recognizing the actions you have taken that are moving your initiative forward, no matter how small.

Some organizations and individuals make the mistake of actively ignoring past achievements as soon as they are completed, focusing entirely on the journey ahead. This is a mistake since our desire to continue on a journey is bolstered when we see how far we have come and our achievements thus far.

As a project manager, one trick that I would use as I updated and posted our project plans was to be sure to maintain a longer-term project plan that showed a few previous months with the completed milestones. This helped me and the team to remember to celebrate what we had achieved, making the journey ahead seem more manageable. I would always make sure that we could see at least one-third of historic effort; this kept our focus on upcoming milestones with a balance of milestones that we could acknowledge and appreciate were behind us. Remember, feeling overwhelmed feeds on a sense of endless work. When the brain sees tangible milestones—a past track record of success—our confidence rises and with it, the belief that we can do it again.

Build Resiliency to Feeling Insignificant

The feeling of insignificance is the feeling like nothing we do matters. Like there is no meaning in it for us. When our daily activities start to feel overwhelming, they can also start to feel senseless. We forget the purpose of the activity, the ultimate good our efforts contribute to. We deem our actions as insignificant in comparison to the challenges, and when our activities lose their meaning, we ourselves feel meaningless. The feeling of insignificance is also isolating. Others around us feel more distant, and we can get a sense that everyone else is moving on a high-speed train that we can't seem to embark on.

Of course, this unpleasant sensation is absolutely in our control to change. It simply requires that we redefine and fully embrace the meaning in our activities. Every task, no matter how mundane, with a little creativity, can be linked to enormous importance.

Make note of every positive contribution your efforts are making to create a positive outcome. Failing to maintain a compelling reason for your activities results in a downward spiral since once our activities are deemed of little importance, so follows our identity.

Being resilient to the sensation of insignificance requires only that you properly honour the energy exerted and the positive contributions you are making. It is built up by focusing each day on augmenting these contributions and noticing their positive impact in the world.

Build Resiliency to Perceived Disconnection

The desire to be connected and belong to a tribe cannot be underestimated. It is primal to every human on the planet. When we begin to slip into isolation, either caused inadvertently by our circumstances or deliberately by our choices or disagreements, we need to realize the potential detrimental effects.

Catching that slipping sensation of disconnection early is at the core of remaining resilient.

The challenge, of course, is that when we begin to feel overwhelmed and insignificant, we often feel much less interesting and engaging. The fact is, we're not feeling great about ourselves, so we judge and criticize ourselves. The orientation towards more judgemental thoughts leads us not only to judge ourselves but also to become more critical of others. This leads us to reject opportunities to be with others since our inner critic deems them not worth connecting with.

The feeling of disconnection is a feeling of closing off, just like not being interested in any fresh air. We shut down our senses, and we literally ignore this very human need, like a plant refusing water. We are declining our own life force and starving ourselves.

Building up our resiliency in this area does require a little bit of subtle awareness. It is frankly difficult to discern the rationality of disconnected behaviours. Our emotional brains easily access painful memories and experiences that tend to validate our apprehension to trust others and limit our desire to connect with them. Connection is a necessary act of vulnerability. It requires allowing yourself to be transparent and seen without any phony facades. In doing so first, we extend an invitation to the other person by creating comfort for them to be transparent as well. Our commitment to them when we open up this connection is to see them as whole (equal and perfect) even with their vulnerabilities, fears and imperfections.

Our emotional mind is not always readily supportive of us taking this risk. It will argue that we are being transparent and open when our behaviour is anything but. That is why I find it more helpful to pay attention to my body since my physiological stress responses don't lie.

Studies of human emotional responses at Aalto University in Finland [26] confirm amazing consistency in the activation of our bodies during emotional experiences, even cross culturally. This means that your body is a great gauge to help you determine 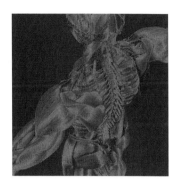 how open you are to connecting with others. One of the key differentiations between pleasant emotions and difficult ones is the sensation in our core area. When faced with negative emotions, the tendency for our bodies is to "go dark", meaning we lose sensitivity almost as though our core centre is deactivated.

Building your own body awareness helps people realize early warning signs of stress (tightened jaw, blushed face, clenched fists, shallow breath)—all signs that they are disconnecting from the other person and entering a fear-based response. Identifying your signs can help you to proactively halt the behaviour by re-engaging yourself in the moment and proactively nurturing your need for connection by switching back to engaging your core and allowing yourself to experience the other person's presence, which is rarely as threatening as we make it out to be.

Build Resiliency to Exhaustion

The final symptom, exhaustion, is easy enough to solve if you are in fact sleep deprived. However, many people experiencing a burnout report feeling exhausted despite the fact that they are getting their required amount of sleep.

What they are experiencing is more accurately described as emotional exhaustion, an even more troubling experience as it tends to be accompanied by an overwhelming lack of vitality.

This final symptom is usually the only physical symptom that individuals attribute to burnout. First warnings of burnout came from the mind (feeling overwhelmed and insignificant), then from the heart centre (disconnection and isolation), and now a full body warning (exhaustion) signalling that the reserves are now fully depleted.

The exhaustion signals the end of the body's tolerance to the environment and forces the individual to stop, prioritizing recovery over all other responsibilities. The recovery at this stage involves a reset and rebuilding from the bottom up, starting with wellness and building up all of the components of the WORK SMART formula.

Resiliency Tip #2: Reduce Your Reactivity

Another important aspect of your resiliency requires developing your ability to reduce your reactivity. Reactivity erodes your resilience like a pickaxe breaking you down while weakening your resolve and consuming your self-management ability.

When I think about self-management skills, I don't think about them as controlling or limiting my reactivity, as many people do. Some believe that self-management is about showing restraint or controlling your reactions rather than altering yourself.

I find using restraint only tires me and my clients. For me, self-management is about choosing better responses, not restraining my response. For that, I like to differentiate between "reacting" and "responding" to a trigger.

I heard a great story that illustrates this concept from Sundar Pichai, CEO of Google. He shared this story [27]:

At a restaurant, a cockroach suddenly flew from somewhere and sat on a lady. She started screaming out of fear. With a panic-stricken face and trembling voice, she started jumping, with both her hands desperately trying to get rid of the cockroach. Her reaction was contagious, as everyone in her group also got panicky. The lady finally managed to push the cockroach away but...it landed on another lady in the group. Now it was the turn of the other lady in the group to continue the drama. The waiter rushed forward to their rescue.

In the relay of throwing, the cockroach next fell upon the waiter. The waiter stood firm, composed himself and observed the behavior of the cockroach on his shirt. When he was confident enough, he grabbed it with his fingers and threw it out of the restaurant.

REACTING VS. RESPONDING
(Trigger)   (Need)

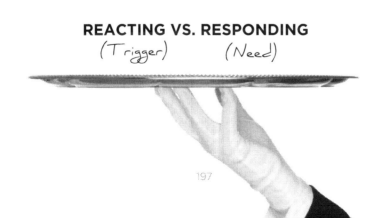

Sipping my coffee and watching the amusement, the antenna of my mind picked up a few thoughts and started wondering, was the cockroach responsible for their histrionic behavior? If so, then why was the waiter not disturbed? He handled it near to perfection, without any chaos.

It is not the cockroach, but the inability of those people to handle the disturbance caused by the cockroach, that disturbed the ladies. I realized that it is not the traffic jam on the road that disturbs me but my inability to handle the disturbance caused by the traffic jam that disturbs me. More than the problem, it's my reaction to the problem that creates chaos in my life. The women reacted, whereas the waiter responded.

Reactions are always instinctive, whereas responses are always well thought out.

Being Responsive

It starts with understanding your common disturbances. I find, there are a finite number of things that generally trigger us in a professional context. These triggers develop over our lifetime, and they are a result of deeply held values or skills that we have worked hard to develop. They are personal to us but are often not shared by others. In fact, that is the problem—they are definitely not universal, which is why others are able to trigger us.

Here is a list of common triggers that you may hold dear. Review the list below and imagine someone challenging you on your...

- Competence
- Authority
- Opinions
- Understanding

- Commitment
- Integrity
- Process
- Policy

You can likely determine your top reoccurring ones that will get a rise out of you more easily. Knowing them is the first step, and recognizing that you are vulnerable to an overreaction when others happen upon them, even by accident, helps you plan for how you will react to them. Such that your reactivity does not get the better of you.

Once you know them, find ways to work through them. Simply knowing them helps, as does visualizing getting triggered and planning the joking or reframing that you plan to do with your response.

Here, I will share three strategies for maintaining your ability to respond that are worth practising. The more you practise them, the more you will be able to navigate through difficult situations and lessen the negative impact of the trigger.

Navigation Strategies

Distance yourself from the comment: This tactic is used to deliberately depersonalize the comment and distance yourself from the situation. Your detachment from the situation helps you manage your emotions and makes the behaviour that is likely to bother you no longer directed at you. This can be done by increasing your attention to positive exchanges, like demonstrated professionalism and appreciation, while disassociating yourself from any incoming negative emotions, like bullying, impatience, anger, or growing frustration. By distancing yourself from the acute situation and holding the deliberate and measured perspective of your best professional self, you can maintain a safe distance between you and any intense emotions that others are exuding.

I learned how to apply this tactic while I was working for a very aggressive client leader. He was a nice man, but he was very insecure, and whenever he interacted with the C-Suite of the company, he became very agitated. As a result, when our project presented our monthly status to the steering committee (made up of the top leaders in the organization), he was difficult to satisfy in preparing for the meeting. To make matters worse, after the meeting, he would raise his voice and shout at me, claiming that I had messed up and should have done things differently. This pattern was damaging to our relationship and unpleasant for me, but I had to work with him and had to endure it. One day when he was shouting at me,

I remembered a scene from The Flintstones where Mr. Slate was yelling at Fred and Fred was shrinking in size. In that moment, I decided to inverse it. Throughout the period of him yelling, I listened to the content but imagined that with every shout, he became smaller and I became larger. This image, and the distance I created for myself, helped me feel strong such that I could capture his needs, and resolve the issues he identified without getting flustered. I even managed to improve our relationship over time due in large part to this technique.

Focus on the desired outcome: Despite what we may think, neurologically, we do not multitask. In fact, our minds are designed with the opposite intent, to dismiss information that is peripheral to our focused activity so that we do not get distracted. When we multitask, we just ask our minds to switch our focus over and over again. This makes multitasking tiring and less effective, but it is also useful for self-management.

When we direct our minds to focus singularly on the outcome we desire, our mind deemphasizes the information related to the trigger. This then diminishes the effect of being triggered. In fact, this is exactly what the waiter demonstrated brilliantly in the earlier anecdote about the cockroach. The waiter's singular focus on the outcome (getting the cockroach out of the restaurant) enabled him to stay calm enough to eject it. When we start with the end in mind and work backwards to determine which thoughts, behaviours, and actions will support the end game, we are much more resilient to threats.

<u>Reframe the information:</u> The third self-management technique requires actively reframing the trigger. What I mean by this is deliberately altering the way you interpret the situation in the moment. I do this manipulation deliberately because I know that if I don't do it, I will be thrown into reactivity and forfeit my opportunity to influence the situation.

Here's an example: In a client workshop with a group of people, there is sometimes an individual or two that may not be enjoying my content. Whether this is just their way of learning or they have a more menacing intention, when they challenge me on the content, it is my responsibility to do my best to meet their needs by responding to their questions while not allowing them to derail the learning experience for others. In the rare instances where I believe that their questions or comments are having a negative impact and becoming disrespectful of the group, I find myself growing impatient and getting triggered. As soon as I recognize that I'm being triggered, I begin to practise rephrasing their questions in my mind before responding. The individual might shout something at me like, "I don't think this applies to my situation at all!" which I will silently rephrase to "What I would really like to hear more about is how this applies to my situation," in a very pleasant tone. That will help me then ask something like "Tell me about a challenge you are facing that you would like to apply this to?" The reframe supports me to respond to the need, not react to their anger or disrespectful tone (the triggers).

Reducing your reactivity starts with knowing your triggers, applying detachment and then reframing the situation to preserve your resiliency in the face of any professional challenge.

Resiliency Tip #3: Create a Prototype to a Better You

In the same way that our minds need to see progress on milestones, our confidence and enthusiasm are bolstered by seeing evolution and progress in ourselves. Resiliency is correlated with our enthusiasm. We have all experienced a time in our lives when we felt so invigorated and completely energized by our experiences that we barely wanted to sleep. Perhaps resiliency is more about building up your desire to be fully engaged and alive than it is about being strong.

To reignite this within us, we need only remember our childhood play habits, the ones we were all born with: the inclination to follow our interests and to chase anything and everything that made us feel curious, interested, or excited. Nurturing this tendency within us can start by asking ourselves these questions:

1. What topics do I feel called to advance?
2. What opinions or judgements do I want to prove wrong?
3. What activities make me feel more vitality?
4. Who inspires me to co-create and experiment?
5. Who do I want to attract to support me?

Once you've done that, it's time to prototype, or what I like to call "play dress up".

First, decide who you need to dress up as to explore all these interests. Step into the role you will assume, and get into action, beginning with experimentation. There's no need to delay or get ready; there's no analysis to do since no historical data can reliably predict your future. The only thing to do is to create-in-action, otherwise known as prototyping, just like this:

1. Pick your first interest area, and figure out physical experiences in the world that would enable you to experiment with it.
2. Pick the first experience and do it, capturing all the insights you can from it.
3. Then take the learning and design your next experience; go for quantity, and go quickly—the more, the better.

Pick your interests and your experiments based on the energy and enthusiasm you feel when you imagine them. You are on the right track when you feel an energy surge with the idea.

This is energy within you that wants to be expressed and will create dis-ease (or worse disease) if you don't use it. Your passion is at the intersection of this energy and a worldly desire or frustration in this moment of time. Let your enthusiasm be your guide, not your intellect, and your resiliency will surge.

Resiliency Tip #4: Keep your Gremlins in Check

Once you are on your way to accelerating your success and prototyping your way to your new future, there's a good chance that your old and familiar mindset gremlins will begin to play some tricks on you. This gremlins surface old thoughts, beliefs and behaviours that threaten your progress.

In Shirzad Chamine's book, Positive Intelligence, he refers to these negative behaviour habits as Saboteurs [28] and covers 10 common saboteurs in his research. I recommend visiting the online resources that Shirzad provides for more details.

I find that most of my clients are sufficiently plagued by 8 gremlins. Gremlins that erode their performance because they attack their Courage, Confidence, Connection and Compassion.

And just like in the movie, these thoughts seem innocent at first, familiar and comfortable, but if you feed these gremlins, they will erode your performance and resilience.

Here's a quick overview of the top 8 gremlins:

GREMLIN	BEHAVIOUR
The Avoider	Thoughts that make you cowardly and convince you to avoid challenging or unpleasant situations
The Worrier	Thoughts that agitate you by highlighting all the dangers you may be susceptible to experiencing
The Hyper-Achiever	Thoughts that cause you to obsess about your achievements and needy for external recognition
The Pleaser	Thoughts that lead you to ignore your own needs because you are obsessed with being liked
The Controller	Thoughts that drive you to be impatient and controlling, damaging to your collaborations
The Hyper-Rational	Thoughts that cause you to dismiss intuition, ignore feelings, overly reliant on linear logic
The Perfectionist	Rigid preferences that cause frustration and resignation in others; which stifles innovation
The Victim	Temperamental thoughts that exaggerate the natural discomfort of growing and learning

Recognizing your gremlins will help you catch yourself eroding your own Courage, Confidence, Connection and Compassion. If you can spot the behaviour, you can stop it. Even under stress, I am now able to catch myself slipping into a worrying hyper-achieving victim. To help you identify your gremlins go to **www.leaderley. com/LeaderleyMindset** for a free assessment.

Now that you can recognize your own thought gremlins, it helps to have a plan for how you will release their lock on your attention. One way to do this is by guiding your thoughts back towards your competencies, your aspirations and elevated identity. Your gremlins will release their hold on you if you do not feed them, by giving them your attention.

Resiliency Tip #5: Intervene Early and Invest in Recovery

Now that you know how to build up your resiliency even in challenging times, you should be able to avoid many unnecessary breakdowns. You will be able to catch the feeling of depletion early and act on it to stay in the game.

I also want to encourage you to consider paying particular attention to signs of mini-breakdowns as these serve as your compass. We all have a tendency to ignore early warning signs as we enjoy bountiful periods in our lives (when things are just working) rather than investing in making important adjustments.

The boom periods of our lives can delight us and distract us from considering the possibility of upcoming challenges. These often prolonged periods of goodness are useful for building up our reserves and making sure that our fundamentals are taken care of.

Don't get me wrong—it doesn't mean you need to worry unnecessarily about when the shoe might drop, but more importantly, you need to think about how to build a solid platform from which you will be able to navigate your future with much more ease. This way, when you experience a bust, it is a very shallow one requiring only a simple course correction and not a deep overhaul.

I recommend being cognisant of investing in your own resilience during good times in three areas: finances, skill building, and health.

The greater a financial buffer you can build for yourself in boom times, the more resilience you will experience. The better maintained your skill sets are, the more durable your success will be when you hit a challenging period. The better your health habits are, the more immunity and physical vitality you will have built up to support you. Ask yourself, "Am I in the midst of a good run now?" Be honest. If so, think about saving some money, investing in your own development and routinizing impeccable health habits.

Conversely, you may be going through an extremely tough time.

When this is the case, get the help you need. Investing in yourself is the best investment you can ever make. It is an act of honouring all that you are.

Many people resist asking for help for too long. They are hard on themselves, believing that they shouldn't need it. This is heresy.

Remember, we are primates, and we need others to support our development. Our recovery and growth is exponentially accelerated with the right entourage. We are wired to help each other and we need to be able to receive help as graciously as we are able to give it.

Find the support you need to master your success rituals and practise self-care that honours your body—the body that is so critical in attuning you to your cumulative wellness and immunity. Your body is, of course, the most complex masterpiece you will ever have the privilege of experiencing; thus, if you care for its needs, it will light up your magnificence. Take the call, meeting its needs—no matter how great or small. Obey it, and make time for it.

Just like Net Present Value calculations discount future dollars to present-day value, the same is true around your Time Value of Excellence. Success compounds itself too, creating a real downside when you unnecessarily prolong your recovery. Prolonged suffering is inept.

If you are in a slump, do not be your own worst enemy. You are absolutely worthy of the investment required to get the help you need. Understand that the most important priority for you when you are in a slump is to get out of it as fast as you can.

Create the environments, invest in support people, and read everything you can that helps you to make progress on yourself every day.

It is through proactive experimentation that you will discover your resilience recipe—the ingredients that you need to keep your body, mood, and mind in optimal shape, which, by the way, is worth its weight in gold!

COACHING EXERCISE

TRIGGERS
Identify your top triggers. I feel triggered when someone questions my:

- ○ Competence
- ○ Authority
- ○ Opinions
- ○ Understanding

- ○ Commitment ○ ....
- ○ Integrity ○ ....
- ○ Process ○ ....
- ○ Policy ○ ....

RECOVERY
How my body reacts when I'm triggered – I feel the following physically:

- ○ Tightened jaw
- ○ Blushed face
- ○ Clenched fists
- ○ Quickening or shallow breath

- ○ Accelerating heart rate ○ ....
- ○ Tunnel vision ○ ....
- ○ Furrowed brow ○ ....
- ○ Raised body temperature ○ ....

Actions that are most effective to help me regain control:

In the moment:

- ○ Deep breathing
- ○ Reframing
- ○ Focus on outcome
- ○ Detach and distance myself

In the near term:

- ○ Exercising ○ ....
- ○ Listening to music ○ ....
- ○ Sleeping it off ○ ....
- ○ Human connection ○ ....

GROWING
Prototyping – I will start to bolster my growth and resiliency:

Prototyping Ideas ....

Inspiring Collaborators ....

Motivating Feelings

- ○ Excited
- ○ Playful

- ○ Inspired
- ○ Curious

- ○ Exploratory
- ○ More fully alive

NOTES

W WELL

O OPPORTUNITY-ORIENTED

R RELATIONSHIP-DRIVEN

K KIND

S SUCCESSFUL

M MANAGERIAL

A ACTION-ORIENTED

R RESILIENT

T TENACIOUS

T

TENACIOUS

Holding Certainty of Outcome in Advance of Evidence

This final and critically important factor in the WORK SMART formula both anchors and bolsters everything we have discussed so far. Tenacity is a quality that powerfully supports us throughout our journey to greatness. We are all born tenacious. Some people neglect to nurture it, but not you—at least not anymore. To know we are born with it, you only need to watch any human baby learn to walk or talk. Our innate tenacity propels us to engage with the world and grow into our bodies without entertaining any doubt that could stop us from trying.

Since our minds need certainty to thrive, it is tenacity that provides that certainty, even when facing uncertain circumstances.

In Angela Lee Duckworth's book, Grit [29], she discusses how perseverance and passion for long-term goals are at the root of this ability. In her research she demonstrates the power of tenacity and suggests that grit is grown from interest, practise, purpose, and hope. I agree with these principles but feel it is important to elaborate in this chapter by providing a few more ideas on how you can grow it.

For starters, to be transparent, I don't love the word grit. Whenever I try that word on, I feel limited, like I have tunnel vision towards a goal. When I tap into my grit, I'm more closed to others and probably harder to collaborate with. I feel a subtle difference when I feel tenacious, like I'm more open to influence, which I believe is important for capturing even greater opportunities.

The more our interests are complex and somewhat ambiguous, which I believe they are in the dynamic world we live in, the more I see that we need tenacity. A tenacious person is clear, determined, passionate, and open.

How do they do that? By tapping into a combination of these seven practices:

1. Apply aspirational thinking
2. Build long-term strategies
3. Grow by taking daily ego risks
4. Be patient, and seek out winning conditions
5. Attract others to your cause
6. Be confident and trust the process
7. Avoid saying no, instead finding a version of yes

Tenacity Practice #1: Apply Aspirational Thinking

The common understanding of the verb aspire is to "direct one's hopes or ambitions toward achieving something" and the root of the word is even more interesting. It comes from the Latin word "aspirare", which means "to breathe upon".

Aspirational thinking therefore has a lightness to it that I believe provides its power. A combination of patience and process are required to achieve worthwhile and challenging goals, which is why tenacity is so necessary. This passion for our goals can also make us frustrated, impatient, and willing to quit. Aspirational thinking takes us beyond goalsetting and into dreaming.

Don't get me wrong—goal setting is important and so is writing them down, in fact. According to Dr. Gail Matthews at Dominican University, you become 42% more likely to achieve your goals and dreams by writing them down on a regular basis. [30] Goalsetting, however, is more of a prioritization process than an aspirational process. Once we narrow in on a goal, we are limiting our focus. Before the narrowing in, there is an important process of dreaming and aspirational thinking is more akin to dreaming.

What I've witnessed in my experience is that when my clients are focused on goals rather than dreams, two things happen. There is a metaphorical clamping down and attachment to the specific attainment of the goal; this brings with it a related tension. I also find that the goals are often more externally focused. In other words, the achievement of the goal is sometimes oriented to satisfying others or gaining recognition rather than intrinsically motivational and sourced by their internal ambition. An achievement ambition that is sourced from a dream maintains its ability for expansion and the ability for the individual to surprise and delight themselves in surpassing any goal. To build this practice I encourage my clients to create and maintain an aspiration list for the sole purpose of expanding themselves. An aspirations list contains ideas, statements or achievements that come to mind when you answer the question: "Wouldn't it be great if?" No timelines, no pressure, no risk of failure – just delightful dreams to activate your prefrontal cortex and expand what might be possible for you.

You know you are on the right track if you get excited at the prospect of achieving a dream, even if no one ever finds out about it.

Of course, people will find out about it, and that is a bonus, but that should not be the source of the ambition or it will not sustain your motivation. To be tenacious requires the interesting combination of internally motivated passion and dedication while maintaining a lightness that provides ample room to grow and expand.

Tenacity Practice #2: Build Long-Term Strategies

Tenacity is not a short-term play. It is a characteristic suited to long-term objectives. Since long-term objectives are harder to specifically nail down, they depend on building a strategy to provide direction. Not having a strategy for your career makes you vulnerable and much more likely to drift in the wind.

That is not to say that you will not end up in good places if you simply drift. For some of my clients, when I start working with them, they share that drifting has worked out just fine for them. They were swooped up, usually quite young, into a current, and they are reasonably happy with where it has brought them. They find themselves surrounded by a supportive and nurturing environment, so they conclude that drifting has worked out just fine.

If you can relate to this, you have been fortunate that drifting has worked out for you, and it may still work out for a period of time. At some point though, most drifters hear a question, intensifying in volume: "Is this it?"

This question will come sooner or later. Some people don't hear it until they are on their deathbed; others hear it when they are 13 years old. The question always comes though, as long as we are drifting. There is something in the human spirit designed to propel us to make our mark, show up as ourselves, and chase our own unique dreams.

I've noticed an incredible difference in my clients' daily motivation after they reflect and build their long-term career strategy. It is like a north star that guides them and makes the near-term milestones somehow seem more fulfilling. Linking your long-term objective to your current activities is transformational.

It stands to reason, then, that specifically identifying what you are tenacious about is fundamental to building your tenacity.

Tenacity Practice #3: Grow by Taking Daily Ego Risks

The third factor in building your tenacity requires getting comfortable with ever-present growing pains. You remember those, right? Those physical aches and pains of growing up, the occasional foot or leg cramp that you had to learn to shake out? None of these were debilitating, but all of them were recognizable and sometimes a little uncomfortable.

Tenacious people learn to love growing pains because they are a recognizable sign of progress. Without the slight discomfort of these recognizable signs, we begin to feel stuck in the status quo, and our doubts grow.

As it turns out, the kind of risk-taking that increases our tenacity is neither physical nor financial risk-taking; it is mostly ego risk-taking. Ego risk-taking occurs when we get over the fear of looking bad in order to fully express ourselves enough to grow. It requires training your ego to stand down so that you can stretch yourself beyond the boundaries of your comfort zone.

If you are not learning and experimenting with new approaches every day, your tenacity will dwindle since your progress will be too slow. Taking the right amount of daily ego risk is no more difficult than constantly trying on new skills. Set a stretch intention for your next meeting. Embarrass yourself a little bit by pushing yourself to the edge of your capabilities.

To help me muster up the courage to take daily ego-risks, I admit I found it necessary to re-brand a number of my feelings. I picked up this idea watching the Olympics. Interview after interview the reporters would ask the athlete just following their event: "Were you nervous?" All of them would reply the same thing: "Not nervous, I was excited though." It dawned on me... They have re-branded feeling nervous as excited. I can do that! I have been re-interpreting my emotions ever since, it is very empowering. Here are some of my favourites ones:

When I feel	I'm actually
Nervous	Excited
Irrational	Innovating
Emotional	Inspired
Embarrassed	Courageous
Confused	Curious
Unprepared	Trying something new
Worried	On the verge of greatness

Wanting to succeed requires being willing to fail. The fastest way to do this is to take risks, capture the learning, and acknowledge your growth regardless of the outcome. This is what growing tenacity enables.

Tenacity Practice #4: Be Patient, and Seek Out Winning Conditions

Tenacity also requires patience—but a very special kind of patience. It is not a passive patience; it is a vigilant patience. This means that every day (or just following a setback) we continue to scan for winning conditions. It requires making small adjustments and trying out your ideas in different contexts with different people while listening for a possible fit.

We are all forced to accept that our timing is not always perfect and that obstacles will arise simply because others may not be ready for our vision.

Tenacious people do not make anyone wrong for not supporting their vision; they just keep iterating the approach, solution, or context, incorporating everything that they learn along the way. When we are patient, curious, and receptive to input—while being vigilant for winning conditions—it feeds our tenacity as the vision of our dream gets sharper and sharper.

Tenacity Practice #5: Attract Others to Your Cause

No one likes to be sold to, especially not to your ideas. People have their own ideas to pursue. That's why tenacity requires that you be eager and driven but perhaps more importantly, happy and attractive at the same time. Being tenacious does not mean that you become demanding or forceful. In fact, it is quite the opposite. A tenacious person is instead charismatic or charming (depending on their preference) and attracts others by inspiring them with their enthusiasm.

When we are charming, we start by appreciating and enjoying what others bring. We allow ourselves to get excited about how their participation will enhance and expand our desires. We invite them to dance with us as we shape the future together. We attract their tenaciousness, which augments our own.

Tenacity Practice #6: Be Confident, and Trust the Process

Tenacity requires us to be certain of the uncertain in the advance of evidence. To do this, we need to be confident but also trust that there is a process at work.

I like to compare this to a field sowed with seeds but with no seedlings in sight. The farmer does not question that some of the plants will yield. He continues to weed and water the soil, trusting that the crop will grow. This analogy applies to your talents and skills. They are your seeds in the ground. They provide all the certainty you need. You need only nurture them and know that with application, they will yield.

I can't tell you the number of times that people compliment me on my courage when I share my story about leaving my corporate job and starting my own business. I can understand their perspective since they appreciate the effort associated with building a brand and a client portfolio as well as developing and delivering services. They also recognize the financial risks involved in giving up a steady paycheck, pension, and benefits.

The hardest part of the journey however was not these things. The hardest part was learning to trust the process as the foundation for my tenacity.

The same applies to you. You have to set yourself on your path, sow your seeds, believe in the quality of those seeds (backed by your talents and skills), and unwaveringly nurture them until they yield a crop. That is what tenacity asks of us.

Tenacity Practice #7: Avoid Saying No, Instead Finding a Version of Yes

Tenacity also requires that we find ways to say yes more often. That we avoid absolute thinking, and that we continuously challenge ourselves to find a path forward from where we are right now.

It is natural to want to plan our journey. We identify the most direct route, and we set out. Yet there will most certainly be road blocks challenging our navigation, and this requires that we be open to detours.

As we approach the detour and evaluate our options, we will certainly feel disappointed that our preferred option is not available. Disappointment is normal but short lived and temporary for tenacious people. Tenacity helps us to create alternatives and pick our preferred option to keep moving.

"No" is a dead end. I work very hard to avoid saying no. I'm not a fan of the expression "If it's not hell yes, it's hell no" or other "no" hype. I encourage a more exploratory and reflective approach since the opportunities all live within a yes; however, it is extremely rare that the offerings will come in the perfect shape. The trick is to figure out how to create the version of yes that augments rather than threatens what is most important to you.

I recommend following these steps to support a dialogue that will either lead to a version of Yes or a very soft No:

Step 1	Appreciate their ask.	A sincere thank you for thinking of you
Step 2	Confirm understanding.	"So if I understand correctly, you want me to…"
Step 3	Be transparent about the issue.	"It sounds really interesting. I would love to find a way to be involved with… I also have this important objective that is extremely important…"
Step 4	Brainstorm win–win solutions with them.	"What if we…" "Might it be possible for us to…"
Step 5	Find the best (even if very small) version of yes from the options.	"How about we…" "What would you think if I…"
Step 6	Make a firm commitment, remain encouraging, and thank them.	"This is what I will do…" "I'm sure we will be able to…" "It's going to be amazing." "Thank you for the opportunity."

Even if the above exchange leads to a soft no, many people find that this method improves their relationships and leads to other open doors.

Tenacity asks us to dialogue and shape opportunities with others, finding a version of yes that complements our intended journey.

Now with these seven practices in mind, your tenacity and confidence in your professional journey will grow exponentially. I also want to remind you, of one more thing that will bolster it further. That is, remembering to celebrate.

Celebrate every achievement (no matter how small or insignificant) acknowledge the progress. Celebrations fortify and secure our tenacity. Our wins weave together like the threads on a very strong rope.

Past successes remind us of how strong we have become and empower us to move forward more boldly with more clarity, determination, passion, and openness.

COACHING EXERCISE

ASPIRATIONS

What is a dream that I stand for?

....

....

What ego risks might I need to take to pursue this dream?
What makes it worth it?

Potential ego risk...

○ Others may not agree with me

○ I could embarrass myself

○ I could fail publicly

○ ....

○ ....

Worth it to...

○ Find others that share vision

○ Express my ideas more fully

○ Accelerate my learning

○ ....

○ ....

ATTRACTING OTHERS

What is so compelling about my vision that will attract others?

About the initiative...

....

....

....

....

About the collaboration...

....

....

....

....

SAYING YES

Where do I want to say yes more, and where do I want to practise more shaping, finding synergies, or delivering a soft no?

Say YES more often:

....

....

....

....

Shape More or Practise Soft No:

....

....

....

....

NOTES

W	WELL
O	OPPORTUNITY-ORIENTED
R	RELATIONSHIP-DRIVEN
K	KIND

S	SUCCESSFUL
M	MANAGERIAL
A	ACTION-ORIENTED
R	RESILIENT
T	TENACIOUS

CONCLUSION

That's it! Now you have it—the WORK SMART formula to unprecedented professional success!

You've made it this far so I'm certain you've found ways to effortlessly create more ease and success in your work. So what's next? Time to make some changes. Don't be afraid of the word "change". Contrary to popular belief, change is easy and exciting!

The reason why change is not hard is because of your mind's neuroplasticity. Your mind is always changing, it is always reprogramming, so all you have to do to change is to try new things and repeat them. The mind knows only repetition.

You are not going to declare a big change—you are going to sneak up on change.

Your brain fights change that is made to seem big or hard. Remember, it is an energy optimizer—it doesn't like the energy required to make big changes, but it doesn't notice small, deliberate shifts in your daily actions. It's used to these changes they occur automatically and easily with each tiny shift in your daily actions.

SNEAK UP ON CHANGE

*"deliberate but tiny shifts
in daily actions"*

So all you have to do is tap into your mind's natural change mechanism by deliberately choosing the tiny shifts that align with your goal.

Now it's time for you to pick some of the tiny shifts that you will deliberately introduce. Here are some examples:

More Well: Write a few positive affirmations that you want to believe, put these on your night table, and read them to yourself first thing in the morning.

More Opportunity-Oriented: In every interaction with your colleagues, try to determine which area of their brain is dominating their thinking patterns. If you notice their primitive brain being activated, try to meet their needs so that their thinking can elevate to their highest level.

More Relationship-Driven: Intentionally consider the health of your most important professional relationships. Each week make it a priority to improve your alignment and shape win–win opportunities with them.

More Kind: Shape a new appreciation ritual at your weekly team meeting. Or experiment with transforming the way you give feedback to others, opting for a fully co-creative process that is free of judgement or criticism.

More Successful: Try role shape shifting your current role. Find ways to spend 15% of your time on areas where you feel uniquely skilled and able to add value.

More Managerial: Identify one neglected but important task that consistently falls off your to-do list, and commit to working on it for 15–30 minutes per day, first thing in the morning, for the next 30 days.

More Action-Oriented: When you feel stuck and unable to take action, recognize it quickly, and spend a few moments untangling the facts from the interpretations that are likely creating confusion or resistance for you. Review the facts critically, and plan only the very next step to get yourself back into action. Remember that failing to take action is the only real failure.

More Resilient: Notice your physical reactions to stress, and develop your ability to de-escalate yourself by intensely focusing on the positive outcome you want to drive in the moment so that you can respond versus simply reacting to the perceived threat.

More Tenacious: Take an ego risk each week by sharing your passions more transparently and seeking the support of others for initiatives that you care about.

Go ahead and pick your top 3 areas and plan a tiny daily action. Track your progress by asking yourself: "Did I do my best today to…?" When the answer is yes, remember to beam with pride! Your brain will absolutely not fight any of these actions and, over a period of time, will memorize and automate them, making them completely effortless. (And then… you will be ready for more!)

I know you have lofty goals, and I'm so excited for you, but don't stress about them. Simply identify the shift you want to focus on and begin today. Don't worry too much. Change is really easy to sneak up on!

WORK SMART—for your vitality, your longevity, and your ability to complete your life's work!

When I started this book, I was focused on documenting all the learnings I have acquired to help you unlock your full potential, get you promoted, and achieve all of your dreams.

I close this book realizing that working smart is so much more important than all of that.

Like so many of you, my family has tragically lost many loved ones too early to cancer, most notably for me personally, my sister Mari-Ellen, the most incredibly talented, engaging, and intelligent woman I have ever known.

When she was diagnosed, she was in her thirties, on top of her game, globetrotting, and enjoying an accelerated career path and the accompanying abundant material perks. She had none of the physiological risk factors: She was in great shape; ate a healthy, nutrient-rich diet; and had no genetic markers or family history. We were perplexed and couldn't understand...why her?

Mari-Ellen wasn't. She was certain she got sick from the stress of working too hard.

I've yet to meet a cancer survivor that does not instinctively understand the link between their work habits and their ability to manage their disease. The illness forces them to attune to the early warning signs and proactively take charge of their habits to not only protect their health but bolster their accomplishments. They realize that achievement at the expense of their vitality is a flawed notion. They know that this is a foolish and unnecessary choice and instead find the synergy between their achievements and working smart in everything they do.

Working smart is not just about accelerating your career (although it will), enriching your life experiences (although it will), and unlocking your potential (although it will); the WORK SMART formula is about your vitality, your longevity, and your ability to complete your life's work.

I invite you to join me on this journey. Challenging yourself to grow and transform into the best version of yourself. Enjoying every inspired step on the journey. I believe with absolute certainty that you can.

IT'S YOUR TURN

Although you now have everything you need to transform your experience at work and accelerate your professional success, you may be looking for ongoing support.

I encourage you to connect with me on LinkedIn and to check out my resources and programs at my website, **www.leaderley.com.** Sign up for leadership coaching tips, complete the WORK SMART assessment at **www.leaderley.com/tools** and consider joining the Kick Start online group coaching program at **www.leaderley.com/academy**.

I also personally deliver executive coaching, training, webinars, workshops, key note speeches and consulting mandates that bring these concepts to life. Our work together will support you and your organization to accelerate your success.

Whether or not you decide to work with me more closely, I want to hear your success stories! I invite you to send me a note telling me how you have applied these tips to accelerate your success. You can reach me at **marisa.murray@leaderley.com**

To your success!

Marisa Murray

ONE QUICK FAVOUR FROM YOU?

I would really appreciate your feedback as I love hearing what you have to say. I also need your input to help me get better and better. Please leave me a helpful review on Amazon at **amazon.com/author/ marisamurray** letting me know what you think of the book. Thank you!

REFERENCES

[1] Lee S Gross, Li Li, Earl S Ford, and Simin Liu, "Increased consumption of refined carbohydrates and the epidemic of type 2 diabetes in the United States: an ecologic assessment", American Journal of Clinical Nutrition, Rockville, MD, May 2004.

[2] Scott Edwards, "Sugar and the Brain", Harvard Mahoney Neuroscience Institute, Dept. of Neurobiology, Boston, 2012.

[3] Chris Crowley and Henry S. Lodge M.D. Younger Next Year, New York: Workman Publishing Company, 2007.

[4] Arianna Huffington. The Sleep Revolution: Transforming Your Life, One Night at a Time, New York: Harmony Books, 2016.

[5] O. Khazan, "Thomas Edison and the Cult of Sleep Deprivation," The Atlantic, Washington D.C., 2014.

[6] Ç. G. B. Ö. Yok Et, "How much information processing the brain," Ciencia em Novo Tempo I. B. University, Madrid, 2010.

[7] Sue McGreevey,"Eight weeks to a better brain," Harvard Gazette, Boston 2011.

[8] D. R. Harris, "The Loneliness Epidemic," University of Bolton, Bolton, UK, 2015.

[9] G. W. Ph.D., "5 Ways Emotional Pain Is Worse Than Physical Pain," Psychology Today, New York, 2014.

[10] Harvard Health Publishing "The health benefits of strong relationships," Harvard Medical School, Boston, 2010.

[11] Andrew K. Przybylski, "Can you connect with me now? How the presence of mobile communication technology influences face-to-face conversation quality" University of Essex, UK, Department of Psychology, 2013.

[12] H. W. a. J. P. Pawliw-Fry, "Performing Under Pressure", New York: Crown Business, 2015.

[13] P. Lainey, "Habiletés politiques dans les organisations," in HEC Montreal, Montreal, 2014.

[14] A. W. W. Malone, "Defend Your Research: What Makes a Team Smarter? More Women," Harvard Business Review, no. June, 2011.

[15] R. E. B. Daniel Goleman, "Social Intelligence and the Biology of Leadership," Harvard Business Review, no. September, 2008.

[16] V. S. G. L. K. R. D. M. Hooker CI, "Neural activity during social signal perception correlates with self-reported empathy," Brain Research, pp. 100-113, 2010.

[17] J. Glaser, Conversational Intelligence, New York: Routledge, 2014.

[18] J. Z. a. J. Folkman, "The Ideal Praise-to-Criticism Ratio," Harvard Business Review, no. March, 2013.

[19] F. Fatemi, "4 Steps To Kill Imposter Syndrome Before It Kills Your Career," Forbes, no. Entrepreneurs, 2017.

[20] C. Lambert, "The Science of Happiness," Harvard Magazine, Boston, 2007.

[21] "Why People Quit Their Jobs," Harvard Business Review, September 2016.

[22] L. Ryan, "Management vs. Leadership: Five Ways they are Different," Forbes, New York, 2016.

[23] American Heart Association Rapid Access Journal Report, "Stress management may enhance cardiac rehab, improve recovery," American Heart Association, Dallas, 2016.

[24] B. Brown, "Gifts of Imperfection", Houston: Hazelden Publishing, 2010.

[25] Business Wire, "The Employee Burnout Crisis: Study Reveals Big Workplace Challenge in 2017," Chelmsford, 2017.

[26] E. G. R. H. a. J. H. Lauri Nummenmaa,"Mapping Emotions On The Body: Love Makes Us Warm All Over," Aalto University, Finland, 2013.

[27] S. Pichai, "Cockroach Theory," LinkedIn, California, 2013.

[28] S. Chamine, Positive Intelligence: Why only 20% of teams and individuals achieve their true potential and how you can achieve yours, Austin: Green Leaf Book Group Press, 2016.

[29] A. Duckworth, Grit: The Power of Passion and Perseverance, Simon and Schuster, 2016.

[30] D. G. Matthews, "Study Focuses on strategies for achieving goals, resolutions," Dominican University of California, Department of Psychology, San Francisco, 2015.

ACKNOWLEDGMENTS

As I embarked on my new career—starting a business and launching my coaching practice—there were so many people who encouraged and supported me.

I would like, in particular, to thank my clients and my collaborators for their confidence and trust in my work.

I also found myself in need of a whole new team of advisors, teachers, and entrepreneurial role models. I would like to acknowledge these individuals for their wisdom and expertise and thank them for generously sharing it with me.

For your positive and lasting impact on me,
I would like to recognize ... (alphabetically)

Angelique Rewers, The Corporate Agent

Ann Gomez, Clear Concept Inc

Brené Brown, Researcher and Storyteller

Chandler Bolt, Self-Publishing School

Jennifer Maagendans, Luna Yoga

Judith Glaser, Benchmark Communications

Marie Forleo, B-School, Copy Cure, and MarieTV

Marilyn Atkinson, Erickson International

Paul McManus, Ana Melikian, and **JoAnne Henein**,
More Clients More Fun

Regena Thomashauer, Author, Teacher, Pioneer

THE 50
WORK SMART
SKILLS

W

O

R

K

About the Author

Marisa Murray has over two decades of success in business and technology leadership roles. A former Partner with Accenture and Vice President at Bell, Marisa built deep strategy, transformation, and change management skills.

As the founding president and chief executive coach at Leaderley International Inc., Marisa supports business leaders to improve their individual and team performance by enhancing their leadership competencies through one-on-one coaching, team coaching and workshops. To see her in action, check out her **TEDx talk: Success without stress** at Ted.com.

She is the author of two Amazon Best Selling leadership books: **Work Smart** and **Iterate!** As well as co-author of the USA Today Bestseller: **The Younger Self Letters**.

Marisa holds her coaching certification with the ICF, is a Professional Engineer and alumni from the University of Waterloo, and holds an MBA from Queen's University. Marisa lives in Montreal with her husband and two sons. Connect with Marisa at **www.leaderley.com**

GIVING BACK

Marisa dedicates 5% of all her revenues to a
for-purpose (not-for-profit) organization.

Her current beneficiary is **www.artistrisud.org**.
An organization dedicated to training entrepreneurial women
in economically challenged regions in the developing world.

Manufactured by Amazon.ca
Bolton, ON